A New and Right Spirit

*Creating an Authentic Church
in a Consumer Culture*

Rick Barger

Foreword by Mark Allan Powell

THE
ALBAN
INSTITUTE
Herndon, Virginia
www.alban.org

The Alban Institute, 2121 Cooperative Way, Suite 100, Herndon, VA 20171

Scripture quotations, unless otherwise noted, are from the New Revised Standard Version of the Bible, copyright © 1989, Division of Christian Education of the National Council of the Churches of Christ in the United States of America and are used by permission.

Cover design: Adele Robey, Phoenix Graphics

Library of Congress Cataloging-in-Publication Data

Barger, Rick.
    A new and right spirit : creating an authentic church in a consumer culture / Rick Barger.
      p. cm.
   Includes bibliographical references.
   ISBN 1-56699-306-7
   1. Church. 2. Christianity and culture—United States. I. Title.

   BV600.3.B377 2005
   262—dc22
                   2004031075

09   08   07   06   VG   2   3   4   5   6   7   8   9   10

Contents

For Mother, whose life and love taught me
faith in a dead-raising God.

Foreword

B efore I was a theology professor, I was a theology student. In 1973 I was a junior at Texas Lutheran College and participated in a class discussion on Paul Tillich. To help us connect with one of that writer's favorite phrases, the students leading our discussion asked each of us to write down what we considered to be our "ultimate concern." Then we went around the room and shared what we had written and why.

Some people had single sentence summaries of a spiritual goal:

"My ultimate concern in this life is to go to heaven and live with God in the next."

"My ultimate concern is to be true to myself as an authentic human being."

Some people identified a primary objective or cause:

"My ultimate concern is to be a witness to the gospel of Christ."

"My ultimate concern is to work for justice and peace in all the earth."

I honestly don't remember what I wrote. I do remember that there was a freshman in the class who had written only one word:

"God."

I also remember that everyone laughed when he read his answer. He was the only freshman in the class and he had not studied as much theology as the rest of us. We told him that God can't be your ultimate concern because *God* isn't something you do or think or say. "Oh," he said. He hadn't understood the assignment.

Thirty years later, I'd like to go on record as saying the freshman got it right. Faith, ministry, Christianity, the church . . . it really is about God. It's *all* about God—it's not about us, not about what we believe or do or think or say, not about the causes to which we commit ourselves or the rituals in which we partake or the doctrines that we profess.

It is ultimately about God, and, to be more specific, it is ultimately about the risen Lord Jesus Christ through whom God comes to us, providing us with goals and causes that may be vital and valid but are not ultimate. Paul Tillich knew this, by the way.

The God who breaks into our lives on Easter morning is both object and subject of our ultimate concern. Everything changed on Easter morning. Something ultimate happened and the church is (no more, no less) the result. The mission of the church is simply to be the result of what God did on Easter. No more, no less.

Some people get this; others do not. Those who get it are not necessarily the wise and the powerful (cf. 1 Corinthians 1:26). They are not always the most charismatic or skillful. They are not necessarily members or leaders of role-model successful churches. But they are invariably participants in the vital transformation that God is effecting in our midst. They are the clearest representatives of what the Bible means by "the church."

I have been to Abiding Hope Lutheran Church in Littleton, Colorado, where Rick Barger is lead pastor, and I know that it is one example of such a church. Abiding Hope was in the news in 1999 when the shootings at Columbine High School shook the lives of their community. They have been celebrated often as a witness to resilient faith; they have been extolled as a congregation that provides a shocking contrast to the modern culture of death and to religion that deals with such a culture on its own terms rather than on the terms defined by God on Easter.

But the miracle that is now Abiding Hope is not a product of Columbine, not a result of unusually effective pastoral care in the face of catastrophic trauma. Indeed, the congregation now is essentially what it was before. Columbine had its effect no doubt, but in a grander scheme it may have been merely the media moment through which the rest of the world recognized what Abiding Hope had going on.

What the media *missed* was that long before the Columbine shootings, Abiding Hope Lutheran Church was a congregation of people who were genuinely excited over God raising Jesus from the dead. What the media *noticed* was simply that after those shootings this was still true.

The real story of Abiding Hope is not what happened in 1999 but what happens every Sunday of the year. One gets a sense of this story simply by walking into the sanctuary any time the congregation gathers. These people are passionate about Jesus, and *as a congregation* they get what faith is all about. It's about God (not them); it's about Jesus Christ, whom God raised from the dead. What happens at Abiding Hope every Sunday of the year seems to be the result of the resurrection.

I have been there, and as near as I can tell, the people of Abiding Hope in Littleton, Colorado do not gather each Sunday to hear inspiring sermons or to experience lively worship or to learn more about the faith or to enjoy fellowship with other believers or to get their spiritual needs met in any number of other ways (though of course any or all of those things might happen). They gather because God raised Jesus from the dead.

What else could they do? God raised Jesus from the dead! How could they (we) *not* gather for worship, for fellowship, for prayer, for proclamation, for celebration of the sacred meal? Such things are results of the resurrection, more outcomes than means to any ends. They are what people do when they discover that God has raised Jesus from the dead.

Abiding Hope is not unique or even exceptional. The church is often cited as exemplary for providing the sort of "adaptive transformational" ministry that is needed in the world today and that is true. They do that. Still, in many ways, and in the most important of ways, I think they are only typical. They are typical of a church that is passionate about Jesus. Perhaps there are too few congregations like that around today—but examples do abound, and they transcend denominational and sociological lines: liberal, conservative, large, small, rural, urban . . . there are vital, healthy, thriving churches that look nothing like Abiding

Hope except in one respect: they are passionate about Jesus, whom God raised from the dead.

Such congregations always have a transforming effect on their own constituency and on the communities in which they thrive. Congregations that are passionate about Jesus become contrast societies not only within the secular culture of our modern times but also within the religious ethos which that culture mistakes for faith. They become contrast societies to any establishment (religious or secular) that thinks in terms of programs and strategies, goals and causes, focusing on what *we* do rather than on what *God* has done. A congregation that is passionate about Jesus becomes a redundant result, being no more and no less than what God creates it to be.

The New Testament identifies the church as "the bride of Christ" (Revelation 21:9; 22:17; cf. Mark 2:19; Ephesians 5:31-33). It is an image that has fallen on hard times of late (perhaps in part due to gender concerns), but I like it. We are identified with Christ via a corporate relationship of passionate love.

It is in reference to this image that I sometimes like to say the mission of the church is simply to love Jesus Christ. Everything else is just strategy. Jesus asked Peter three times, "Do you love me?" and told him three times, "Feed my lambs; feed my sheep" (John 21:15-17). Feeding sheep is important. It is one of the many important things that Jesus wants the church to do. But Jesus doesn't just want the sheep to be fed; he wants them to be fed by those who love him.

What do people who love Jesus do? They feed his sheep. They also keep his commandments (John 14:15, 21; 1 John 2:5; 5:3) and are attentive to his word (John 14:23, 24). They serve the saints (Hebrews 6:9) and love all of God's children (1 John 4:20–5:2). They show mercy (Matthew 5:7) and make peace (Matthew 5:9). They rejoice with indescribable and glorious joy (1 Peter 1:8). I'm sure we could come up with a long list of activities and qualities that the scriptures indicate should be attributable to people who love Jesus—and then we would have a list of strategies, an account of suggested ways for us to express this love that defines us.

If loving Jesus is the *essence* of the church's mission, it is also its *identity*. Peter practically defines the church as people who love Jesus Christ (1 Peter 1:8), indeed as people who do so as a result of a new birth through which God brings them "into a living hope through the resurrection of Jesus Christ from the dead" (1 Peter 1:3).

Likewise, I'm not sure that brides and grooms think of loving each other as a mission, as something that they are *supposed* to do. It is that, but they might think of it more naturally as basic to their identity—it is what brides and grooms typically do. They love each other, passionately, and strategize to find frequent and appropriate ways for expressing that love. And though some couples may benefit from suggestions regarding the best ways for demonstrating love, few would benefit from such counsel if the love were not there to begin with.

So Rick Barger links the creation of an authentic church in our consumer culture to the cultivation of a *right spirit*. The congregation that is in a corporate relationship of passionate love with Jesus Christ whom God has raised from the dead can learn strategies for demonstrating that love in a postmodern world. Indeed they will typically do so. But the spirit must be there, the resurrection spirit of living hope that makes the church to be what God creates it to be.

This "right spirit" is what people notice first at Abiding Hope—not programs or mission directives, but a spirit of life that arises from what God did on Easter morning. Perhaps the greatest gift of Abiding Hope to Littleton and to the world is simply that one finds there a gathering of people who are passionate about Jesus and excited that God has raised him from the dead. The enthusiasm is contagious; the right spirit spreads. Identity and mission merge, for as Rick Barger says, the most important task for the church right now is simply for the church to be the church, the redundant result of Easter, the passionate people whom God has brought into being by raising Jesus from the dead.

Mark Allan Powell
Trintiy Lutheran Seminary, Columbus, Ohio

Acknowledgements

I am grateful to the Alban Institute for their willingness to publish this book; my experience with them has been both humbling and inspiring. I am especially grateful to David Lott, who was managing editor of Alban when I signed my contract. David not only persistently believed that my voice needed to be heard through Alban; he also stuck with the project and with me after leaving his post with Alban. David's insights, his willingness to challenge me and ask hard questions, his penchant for clarity, and his gifts for written expression were all invaluable to the process. He was particularly patient with me when I had to put the manuscript on hold after my mother suffered a massive stroke and during those six months when my wife and I provided care for her until her death.

I am also grateful to Mark Allan Powell, Walter Bouman, and Allen Sager at Trinity Lutheran Seminary, who encouraged me to publish my cultural and ecclesiological take on the church. During the writing of the manuscript, several people took the time to review the working manuscript and give me their feedback. I am particularly thankful to two former pastoral residents, Paul Mussachio and Nathan Swenson-Reinhold, who served under my supervision and gave thorough critique of my work. I am also grateful to my two pastoral colleagues, Doug Hill and Chad Johnson, who also participated in reviewing my work. Leonard Sweet was helpful in pushing me to grab and develop the "re-conceiving" metaphor for the church to the extent that I was riding the "re-orientation" metaphor. Another valuable assist goes to my wonderful wife, Harriet. Not only did she give me the space I needed to write this book, she also took the time to lend her watchful eye to the manuscript and to ask needful questions of it.

Most of all, I will always be thankful to the congregation I serve, Abiding Hope Lutheran Church, its leaders and its staff. They both encouraged me to write this book and graciously gave me the time and space to do it. Collectively, these people of God with whom I share the overwhelming majority of my life are incredibly gifted by God and are the most authentic and hopeful folks I know. What I learned through this whole process is that no one publishes a book, even a rather small one like this one, without the help and partnership of many.

The Quest for Authenticity

On the front door of our house hung a little white plastic bag containing a videotape. Its cover showed a picture of an immensely obese sumo wrestler who hung suspended in the air, his legs split, almost parallel to the ground as if he were a gymnast. His right arm was stretched straight up over his head and his hand was palming a basketball. He was a four-hundred-pound Michael Jordan! Under this picture were these bold words: "Just imagine." In smaller print were these words: "7 minutes."

So what the heck? Not knowing who hung this curious tape on my door nor what it was about, I turned on our television, cued up the VCR, and inserted the tape. Almost immediately the room was filled with upbeat music. On the screen appeared a video shot zooming in on the new church facilities of a nondenominational megachurch located on the perimeter of our neighborhood. The audio portion began with the words, "Just imagine." What unfolded over the seven minutes was very clever and inviting. Filled with scenes of smiling and happy people, the tape asked me, the viewer, to just imagine a gorgeous place with all kinds of wonderful programs. A place with programs for small kids, junior high kids, and high school kids. A place with programs for married couples and programs for singles. A place with programs for small groups, not to mention worship programs. Each of these programs promised excitement, meaning,

1

and fun. I, the viewer, was then invited to come to the grand opening of this place.

What unfolded on this seven-minute tape was not unlike another videotape that I had received some time ago. This other tape was from Sandals, a small chain of couples-only resorts located in various places in the Caribbean. My wife and I had celebrated thirty years of marriage by spending a week at a Sandals resort in Jamaica, and they were now offering a special deal to generate more repeat customers. This tape also had all kinds of smiling and happy people. It, too, promised a gorgeous setting with all kinds of exciting and fun-filled programs.

The similarities between these two videotapes and the experiences they were selling ought to cause us to pause and reflect upon how our market-driven culture perceives the nature and purpose of the church of Jesus Christ, the one who was crucified and is now raised. I am not putting down this church videotape nor questioning the sincerity of the congregation who distributed it. In terms of ingenuity and probable expenses incurred, it exceeds anything my congregation has ever done to reach out to our community. It was such a local marketing hit that many people in my congregation found it necessary to share their copy with me. "Did you see this? You really need to see this! It's good! We ought to do something like this." I raise the striking similarities between these two tapes and the affirmation the church tape received in my own church community to illuminate a critical challenge the church faces in our North American, twenty-first-century context: the church and the culture in which it exists are both confused about the church's identity and calling.

Given the market-driven and consumer-based realities of our world, the church too often comes off, or is perceived, as some sort of spiritual version of a community recreation center, simply offering up programs and experiences to meet people's needs. That the church has a story to tell—a true story!—that makes outrageous claims about God and God's relationship with the world and all of humankind is obfuscated in the midst of this confusion. Imagine instead the reaction to a marketing piece that said something like this: "We invite you to come to our congregation. Here you will be immersed in a story that exposes much of what our world has handed to you about human life—its values and its purposes—as lies, declares our world and all of its schemes dead, and promises to put you to death and raise you to new life. You will be so grasped by this story and pulled into our congregation that lives out of this story that you will one day find yourself at odds with the values, attitudes, and priorities of many of your neighbors and maybe even your own family."

I have no idea about the kind of traction such a candid marketing piece would have in our culture. Would it be, from a business standpoint, a colossal failure, or would it be, for some, a breath of fresh air? The societal tension in which the church lives is that, on the one hand, our culture is conditioned to respond to gimmickry, simple answers to complex issues, and offers of instant gratification; yet, on the other hand, we have a deep longing for authenticity, in whatever form it may exist.

As we have crossed the threshold of a new millennium, the main calling of the church is not a matter of more programs, more strategies for membership recruitment, and more ways to meet people's needs. It is a matter of *authenticity*. It is about being clear with the very story and its claims that gave birth to the church and continue to give it its life. It is to bring light to age-old questions: Who are we? In what do we hope? What are we to do, and how shall we live?

A Hopeful Time to Be the Church

My guess is that if you have picked up this book to read, you probably love the church. You likely are a pastor, a paid or unpaid servant-leader in your congregation, a seminary student preparing to answer God's call to you in the church, a seminary teacher, or you hold some other position of servant-leadership in the church. Because you are who you are, you must have a fascination with the God in Jesus Christ whom the church proclaims and is invited to follow. I assume that you hold the gospel—that is, the good news of the life, death, and resurrection of Jesus Christ—to be the most compelling and urgent message in our world today. And I suspect that you sometimes stumble over the church's gospel and at other times find it as delightful foolishness in an insane world that serves other messages.

Because you do serve the church in some way, I genuinely hope you share in what I passionately believe: this is a great time to be the church. For sure, all of us are aware of distressing studies and reports that are filled with bad news about the church. Mainline Christianity in North America continues to falter. Too many congregations are supposedly in decline or near death. Too many people who serve the church suffer from burnout. Too many congregations are engaged in divisive and soul-killing conflict. And then there is the public awareness of clergy misconduct that raises questions about the church's trustworthiness. At the same time, the spirituality and self-help sections comprise the largest sections in our communities' big chain bookstores. That these sections are located next to each other tells us that people see religion or spirituality as akin to self-improvement. That, in and of itself, should give us clues to the challenges the church faces in its quest for authenticity. Multiple studies confirm that North Americans overwhelmingly believe in God, yet many have chosen not to belong to a community of believers. As with everything else in American life, we Americans will do things "our way."

And yet we live at a time in the church when there are all kinds of reform movements going on. Every church body has some movement of reform. In the last quarter of the twentieth century the church-growth movement was born, a reform movement that seeks to revitalize the church through attracting people into the church by identifying their needs and meeting them. The church-growth movement has found its way and taken root in some manner or another in just about every church body. Within my church body, the Evangelical Lutheran Church in America, there are several grassroots efforts that use the word *transformation* in one way or another to describe themselves. It is a rare week when we pastors do not have a flyer cross our desks inviting us to a conference on how to revitalize or reinvent our congregations or to a seminar on clergy renewal or leadership development (indeed, the congregation I pastor has its own leadership academy and hosts other conferences throughout the year). These are always well attended—a sign of the interest these days in such matters. And pastors, church workers, and seminary students would have to be on another planet to avoid the critically necessary conversations about the transitions, challenges, and opportunities the church faces in having left the modern age and now entered into the postmodern world.

I hear the cries of despair about the state of the church and view the multiple movements toward reform as signs that God is again reviving God's people. Frankly, I have little tolerance for those who hold court on the church and bash its leadership. But I also am suspicious of one-size-fits-all strategies that promise to fix any struggling congregation. I experience all of what is going on in the church through the metaphor that belongs to the baptized—being put to death for the purpose of being raised to new life. My soul tells me that God is up to something right now in the North American church. The result will be the emergence of a renewed and contextually relevant church that is vibrant, life giving, and contagiously attractive because of its authentic passion and hopefulness. One of the biggest pieces of evidence that points to my ardent belief that God has not given up on the church and in these days is truly up to something is my experience of the high quality and character of those individuals whom God has called into service in the church—you! You, the readers of this book, are the evidence of God at work. So with these assumptions about who you are, I hope you will experience this book as exceedingly hopeful. I intend for it to be that way. After all, how can we not be unashamedly hopeful when we have been grasped by a special community whose very life emerges out of the joyous cry, "He is risen!"?

Searching the Church's Inventory

To be clear about the personal orientation I bring to this book, I am not writing this book *at* the church. I write this book *to* the church and from *within* the church, as a lifelong child of the church. I have been richly blessed, healed when broken, challenged, and transformed by the church and its story. When many of my boomer generation left the church, I did not. I have not always been a pastor, but even before I left my first career to go to seminary, I never left the church. Therefore, before you get too far into reading this book, I need to warn you: there is not one original idea in this book.

There is not one original idea in this book because we already have the DNA for reconstructing an authentically transformational church. It is in our inventory—our inventory of the grounding proclamation of the church, the scriptures that bear witness to our God, and our liturgies born out of the primal days of the church.

It is told that William Randolph Hearst, the wealthy California newspaper magnate, once deeply desired a particular painting. So profound was his desire for this painting that he dispatched members of his staff to search the globe for it. They looked on every continent, visited hundreds of galleries, interviewed countless curators and collectors, and in the end, they failed to find the painting. In despair, Hearst stubbornly called off his search and resigned himself to the reality that he would never be blessed by this work of art. Some time later, after his death, an inventory was taken of all the paintings and artwork he had stored in his basement. To everybody's surprise, the very painting for which Hearst had hungered was found among his inventory. That for which he searched he already had.

I owe much of the inspiration for my thinking about the church to Loren Mead, founder of the Alban Institute and the author of *The Once and Future Church*.[1] Mead and other works in an Alban series[2] under "The Once and Future Church" rubric argue that the "crisis" the church faces has to do with the church's relationship to its "mission." To paraphrase Mead, there is something fundamentally flawed about the way the church does church. I would prefer to use the word *calling* rather than *mission* as the core problem, but I believe Mead's diagnosis is essentially correct. Mead points to the collapse of the Constantinian synthesis (more on this below) as the cause for the "crisis" in the church today. This collapse is not something to be lamented but is rather something to be celebrated. The Constantinianization of the church was actually a hijacking of the church's identity and mission. What initially may have seemed like great news to the Christians in the Holy Roman Empire actually turned out to be not just a terrible idea for the European church but also ultimately for the entire church—West and East. This bad idea still so casts a spell on the American experience of the church that it would be impossible to overstate the effect Emperor Constantine and his successors had on the church. Perhaps an abbreviated historical tour of the church and the culture might be useful here.

The Constantinian Synthesis

From its very birth, the church understood itself to be a contrast society. Some Christians took this notion to the extreme, forming groups who retreated from the norms of life in the ancient world and lived in isolation. The vast majority, however, lived and worked among the rest of the citizenry of the Roman Empire.[3] The distinction between the church and the social world in which it lived was clear to the church. Christians organized their lives and life together around the implications of the meaning of the church's primal claim: Jesus of Nazareth, the one who was crucified, is now raised from the dead. The event of Jesus is not just something that God did *for* the world. It is also something God did *to* the world. The church thus had its own narrative, a story in sharp tension with the cultural narrative of the world around it: Jesus, not Caesar, is Lord. The church knew its identity to be given in baptism, whereby members are joined to Jesus Christ and his death and resurrection. It understood its calling in the world to be to bear witness as a sign of the changed condition of the world and its promised future wrought through God's action in Jesus Christ. It forged its identity and calling weekly as it gathered for worship on Sunday, the day of Jesus' resurrection. The church experienced the living Christ's accessibility and availability through its liturgy, its life together, its posture of hopefulness, and its modeling of Jesus' healing and merciful compassion for the world.

In the apostolic era of the church, the boundaries between the church and the Empire culture were clear and distinct. To use biblical language, the church was "in the world but not of the world." As history shows, not much time elapsed before the church lived in an environment that was hostile to it. To be loyal to Christ must mean to be disloyal to Caesar, and disloyalty to Caesar meant persecution and sometimes death.

In 313 c.e., beginning with the quasi-conversion of Emperor Constantine, the relationship between the church and the world around it would begin to change completely. It was as if a massive tidal wave had washed over the church and the culture, wiping out boundaries and leaving a totally new landscape. Emperor Constantine believed in the power of Christ, but he believed in a way that was quite different from the Christians who were earlier persecuted. Constantine had an agenda. He believed that the Christian God was a powerful God who would support him and give him an advantage over his enemies. His aim was to enlist the Christian God into service of him and his empire. Constantine quickly made Christianity the religion of the Roman Empire. His vast program of building churches, enacting laws that supported Christianity, inculcating the Christian faith into education, making sure that each village and city celebrated the major Christian festivals, and enmeshing the office of emperor with the leadership of the church were all motivated out of a pre-enlightenment cause-and-effect mind-set. These things would pay off with good things for him and for the Empire.

Of course, who can argue with much of the good that Christianity did do for the Empire? People were taught the basic Christian story. They learned the creeds. They learned concepts like sin and forgiveness, unconditional love, charity, kindness, and other attributes of living the Christian life. More importantly, they worshiped, heard sermons, and were fed at the Eucharist. Monasteries took in people who would devote their whole lives to following Christ, preserving the scriptures and the biblical languages, articulating theology, and working to better the world in which they lived. The Christian story inspired artists, architects, musicians, and writers that gifted the world with magnificent works. Much more could be cited here, but suffice to say that Christianity did gift the world with much good.

Nevertheless, the Christianization of the Empire under Constantine meant a reinvention of the church's identity and calling. This reinvention would ultimately prove to be disastrous for the integrity and spiritual power of Christianity. The hostile boundary between the church and the culture disappeared. The church became a partner in the culture. This new partnership meant that the sacred narrative of the church merged with the narrative of the Empire. There was no longer "one Lord, one faith, one baptism, one God and Father of all" (Ephesians 4:5-6) that defined a church in tension with the culture. There was now one empire and one story. The stories were so intertwined with one another that emperors and political leaders would take a full role in the development of the church, and church leaders would often engage in political and military leadership.

Except for certain religious minority groups who lived in the Empire, such as Diaspora Jews (Jews who left Palestine under Roman conquest, occupation, and attempts at expulsion), there was no distinction between being a Christian and being a member of the Empire. The boundary between the church and the world evaporated, and a new distinction emerged. Instead of the church existing as a contrast society within the Empire, the new enmeshed partnership of church and empire defined itself over and against the geopolitical world around it. This meant a transformation in the understanding of mission. Mission was directed at the conversion and, sadly, sometimes at the conquering or destroying of pagans beyond the Empire's perimeter or on its fringes. Within the boundaries of the Empire, the church's role became that of a religious chaplain to the culture. Being in partnership with the Empire, the church went about the business of brokering with God the salvation of the souls of the Empire and providing the Empire and its citizens with religious support and services. This discussion is not to suggest that there were not times of great tension and struggles for power within the church and between the church and political leaders. Nor does this address the issues of corruption and some of the church's shame-

ful initiatives that are part of European church history. The point
here is that the Constantinization of the church worked to put
the church and the world in such an enmeshed relationship that
the church's story and the Empire's story were indistinguishable
from one another.

When Europeans first began to immigrate to America they
brought their Constantinian mind-set with them; yet, at the same
time, they did not want to replicate the marriage of empire and
religion. Radically breaking from their European roots, the authors of what would become the Bill of Rights—that is, the first
ten amendments to the Constitution of the United States—for-
bade in 1789 the establishment of any national religion. Any
assumption that the new nation was to identify itself with any
single form of church or religion was, in effect, constitutionally
disestablished. That was what was on paper. In actuality, the
emerging nation, which was to become the United States, inherently understood itself not only to be Christian, but, for the first
two centuries, essentially *Protestant*-Christian.[4] The pinnacle of
this self-understanding was perhaps the experience of World War
II and the decade of the 1950s that followed. From the American perspective, the war was clearly a war in which God had to
be on the side of America. Church attendance flourished, not
only during the war but also in the years following. New opportunities and economic expansion gave way to a very optimistic
outlook toward the world. God was good. Bibles were read in
public schools. Prayer before assemblies and football games was
expected. Blue laws were in effect. Stores, theaters, and most other
establishments were closed on Sundays. Community calendars
aligned with the calendars of the local churches. In the south
and midwest, Wednesday nights were usually protected as nights
reserved for church activities. Schools would not even think of
having parent-teacher conferences on the same night as Maundy
Thursday, a conflict that occurs with some frequency today. The
question of church identity in the 1950s was not about whether
or not one was a Christian. That was simply a given. The real
question was to what Christian denomination one belonged.
Except in certain locales, the world of Judaism generally kept a

very low profile. Buddhism and other religions belonged to certain ethnic groups who lived in identifiable enclaves in the major cities. From a wide-angle and big-picture point of view and in the consciousness of this country, America was Christian.

The Constantinian Synthesis and the
Second Half of the Twentieth Century

Sometime in recent history, the enmeshed relationship between the church and the culture began to become unraveled. Theologians Stanley Hauerwas and William Willimon date the appearance of the first cracks to be around 1960.[5] The beginning of the unraveling coincided with the genesis of the tumultuous events that define the generational experience of the baby boomers, that huge group of some seventy-six million people born between 1946 and 1965. Their attitudinal and worldview-shaping generational experience became known as "the Sixties." "The Sixties" is capitalized and in quotations here because it does not precisely refer to the decade of the 1960s. Rather, it refers to an experience and cultural transformation, a good part of which actually happened in the 1970s. "The Sixties" began with the assassination of President Kennedy in November 1963 and ended with the resignation of President Nixon in 1974 following the Watergate scandals. In between was the experience of the war in Vietnam, which not only deeply divided the country but also divided many boomers from their parents. It was marked as well by the civil rights movement (along with its strife and unrest), the assassinations of Martin Luther King Jr., Bobby Kennedy, Malcolm X, violent riots at the 1968 Democratic convention in Chicago, and the Arab oil embargo of the early '70s that led to a major recession. It also saw the sexual and gender revolutions, the rise of a drug cult, the Beatles, the Rolling Stones, Bob Dylan, and Woodstock, a weekend rock concert that served to define the collective, in-your-face personas of what seemed like the vast majority of boomers.

Out of "the Sixties" experience emerged some major shifts in boomer attitudes and beliefs, not the least of which included a new skepticism toward institutions and any claim of universal truth, as well as a resistance to conformity, that would ultimately define and give new shape to the American experience.[6] These shifts also served to prompt a boomer exodus from the church. Not all boomers left, but many who did left because of frustration over the church's ineptness in dealing with issues of deep importance to them, such as civil rights and the threat of nuclear annihilation. Others drifted away from the church, not out of some conscious decision to leave but because the church just simply floated off of their radar screens. The church was no longer relevant to them.

It is perhaps one sign of God at work in today's world that many boomers are choosing to return to church. Religious researcher Wade Clark Roof extensively studied the boomer relationship with the church. In 1993, he wrote that 25 percent of the boomer generation were returnees to the church.[7] Perhaps today that percentage has increased. In the congregation I serve we continue to receive into membership large numbers of boomers who are returning to the church after a prolonged absence. As Roof suggests, they return with an agenda. They are searching and seeking. Perhaps they come because of a midlife crisis. Perhaps it is due to an awareness of the uncomfortable dissonance between the realities of their outer lives and the core values of their souls, and they come seeking something that will give them resonance. Perhaps it is because they desire religious teaching for their children. As I listen to people who enter into our new-member preparation process I hear these reasons:

- "I am looking for community."
- "In these tumultuous times, I am looking for something in which to anchor my life."
- "I have discovered that material things have not brought me happiness and I am spiritually searching."
- "I am afraid of the world in which my children are growing up and their exposure to violence, greed, and sex, and I want to give them a foundation."

No matter how people enter the church in this boomer-shaped culture, you can be almost certain of one thing: they will enter the church from the posture of being a consumer. In their book *Shopping for Faith: American Religion in the New Millennium*,[8] Richard Cimino and Don Lattin expose that which all of us who serve the church know: folks enter the church's doors today shopping for faith. They unashamedly admit that they are "church shopping." They are searching for something. They seem to know what they want, or at least intuitively believe that when they stumble upon that for which they are searching, they will know it. They have no trouble mixing traditions. That is, one person might join a Presbyterian church because he likes the pastor and yet still clings to some of his Roman Catholic upbringing, or another person might affiliate with a Lutheran church because she is drawn to a particular contemporary worship service and its close proximity to her home, yet she reframes all of the "grace alone" preaching through the filters of her Southern Baptist upbringing and the conservative Bible study group she attends weekly. Yet another might worship in an Episcopal Church because of a love for the liturgy and at the same time practice some of the spiritual disciplines of Zen Buddhism. The point here is that they have deep perceived spiritual and personal needs, and they are determined to get their needs met. If they do not, they are going to go someplace else. They are going to have it their way. And it seems that there are an infinite number of choices. After all, if you can go into Starbucks and choose from countless permutations and combinations on how to have a cup of coffee, why can't you do the same thing when it comes to being affiliated with a faith community?

The Collapsed Constantinian Synthesis and Cultural Confusion

The unraveling of the Constantinian synthesis and the consumer-driven realities of today's world bring us to the conundrum that the church faces today—Mead's "crisis." The Constantinian synthesis is over. Though there are some living relics from that era that would suggest otherwise, such as "In God We Trust" on our currency, it is absolutely clear that not all Americans share a collective, single view about issues of faith—not between the church and the state, not between the church and the public, not between neighbor and neighbor, and not even between people sitting next to each other in the same pew. This reality was especially evident in the recent election of George Bush over John Kerry, an election in which the Wednesday-morning quarterbacking that followed it kept noting the great division over faith and values among the electorate. The age of religious pluralism is here—both in a multiplicity of world religions and the prevalence of pluralism within the various faiths, including Christian pluralism. Therefore, when President Bush led a national worship service on the Friday following the events of September 11, 2001, in order to be inclusive, he called upon a Jewish rabbi, an Islamic cleric, and a Christian pastor to address the nation collectively. And those within Christianity, probably as well as the other faiths represented, were not even on the same page as to the one who should represent them that day. Many Christians asked, "Does Billy Graham really speak for me?"

Raising again a question from the opening pages of this book, is it any wonder then that people live in a state of confusion over the identity and calling of the church? Loren Mead says that the church today exists within a context of ambiguity. The culture is a mixture of openness, indifference, confusion, and hostility toward the church. It is my experience that most people enter the church not knowing just what the church is and its purpose—its identity and calling—or the notion they have is misinformed. I experience the same confusion over the person of Jesus. I now assume that people either do not know who Jesus is or the assumption they have about Jesus is off target. I am even no longer surprised when we receive lifelong members of the church into our membership preparation process, people who are well educated, culturally sophisticated, and successful by the world's standards, and we experience them as biblical, theological, and ecclesiological infants or adolescents.

That we live in an age of ambiguous cultural perceptions toward the church within a reality of religious pluralism means that the church has to work very hard at being clear about its own witness to the world. Such required definition cannot emerge from a posture of religious or theological elitism. Religious pluralism is a fact of contemporary life, demanding that the church be both open and honest about different expressions of faith and that people will conflate differing traditions to meet their own perceived needs. It is therefore unproductive energy for the church to blame religious pluralism for the challenge the church faces today. It is also unproductive to blame the confusing and complex cultural realities. No one is to blame. The challenge the church faces is that its own unique gift to the world—its ancient and authentic story of Jesus Christ, crucified and risen, and the implications of that story—lies under the clutter of a very complex matrix of religious pluralism, market-driven realities, and the symptoms of a church and culture both suffering from a hangover from the Constantinian synthesis.

No More Playing on Astroturf

A lot of football and baseball in this country is played on synthetic turf. For whatever reason the owners of some stadiums have made the choice that synthetic turf is preferable to real turf. The decision is often entirely economic. Never mind that synthetic turf causes more injuries. Never mind that synthetic turf is disdained by football and baseball purists. Synthetic turf requires much less care and maintenance than the real stuff. Synthetic turf requires no gardener. Synthetic turf has no soil.

The future hope of the church lies in the rich soil of the church's authentic and ancient story. To recover and appropriate that story and put it authentically to work in a transforming congregation means also to recognize that much of the church and culture today are playing on Astroturf. Though the Constantinian synthesis has collapsed, we still suffer from a Constantinian hangover. The Constantinian hangover means that Astroturf has been used to pave over and obscure the ancient and authentic story of the church and its cosmic-rattling implications. If the church is perceived as essentially being on the same page as the culture, then other than periodically serving as the culture's conscience, what does the church really have to offer?

Under the Constantinian synthesis the church did not offer a radically alternative story. Rather, it offered deals, causes, and spiritual services. The prime deal was the deal of salvation. Playing ball under the right rules with the church insured eternal seating rights in heaven. By the end of the sixteenth century, you could actually purchase your seats through the sale of indulgences. Of course, in order for the church to have the audacity to try to get away with selling indulgences, the church had to reinvent God completely. God was made over into One to be greatly feared. God was given credit for awful things like the bubonic plague and pictured as One who had no trouble casting into the eternal fires of hell a poor lost soul on the basis of the slightest indiscretion. God still suffers in some circles from this despicable misrepresentation.

A prime cause the church took up for the Empire was the crusade to wipe out the Muslim infidel in the Holy Land, a cause declared to be the divine will of God. People were expected to support such a cause through either marching off to the Holy Land themselves or through prayer and sacrifices that supported the efforts. The spiritual services the church offered included the disbursement of selections from the church's menu of sacraments. There could be a private Eucharist performed on behalf a loved one, dead or alive, or the performance of last rites, the last service before death. Priests were often consulted and freely gave their guidance or instructions on any aspect of life.

Because the rich soil of the church's authentic witness has been undercultivated and because of the market-driven aspects of the culture today, the church seemingly continues to be stuck in a perception that its role is either about deals, causes, or spiritual services. There are expressions of the church that are adamant that the sole purpose of the church is to broker the deal of eternal salvation with as many people as possible. They are very clear and specific on what the terms of the deal are. But there are also other deals disclosed by the rhetoric often coming from the church: "Take part in this program and you will become a better parent or a better leader." "Come and worship with us and we guarantee you an uplifting experience."

The church also still enlists people in causes, such as, "We need you to help feed the hungry" or "We need for you to help us provide a place for our youth." In times of war, some churches post the American flag in their worship spaces, suggesting that worship of God is likewise supporting an American cause. Almost all deals and causes have the added incentive of promising that "it will be meaningful," tapping into an especially deep longing for the bored, empty, and searching. There is nothing wrong with wanting to be a better parent, feed the hungry, provide a safe place for kids, or offer prayer on behalf of our troops and our country's leaders, but these pursuits must be given their life through the rich soil of the church's grounding story. When the church's authentic story lies obscured below the surface, disconnected from the congregation's life, the church is playing on Astroturf. It may look like church, but it's more artificial or superficial than the real stuff. Little wonder, then, that many perceive the church as a purveyor of religious programs or some sort of spiritual services—a reality with which every pastor struggles.

The church is not its programs, schemes, deals, or causes. It is not aligned with any national agenda. The church is a contrast people society, created and sustained by God through the crucified and living Christ. The challenge that the church faces is to simply be the church. As William Willimon and Stanley Hauerwas argue in *Resident Aliens*, the gospel of the crucified and living Christ proclaims that the world created out of our imaginations, with our deals and causes (my words), is actually dead.[9] That world is over. The church is the living sign—the living witness—of the brand-new world given and promised by God. The taproots of that new world run deep into the grounding story of the church. There is no Astroturf.

In the church's inventory, then, is this rich soil that once gave birth to the body of Christ and powerfully shaped its life. There are some congregations who have refused to allow that soil to lie dormant. They have found great renewal and vitality by finding their way through the cultural and ecclesiological clutter in order to position themselves upon, and get their life from, the rich soil. These congregations are advance scouts for an emerging authentic and transformational church in today's world. Inspired by these congregations and following the clues offered by Loren Mead, the central thesis of this book is that church vitality is finally about *authenticity*. Authenticity is not about replicating a first-century church and relocating it to the twenty-first century. Authenticity means to take seriously the ancient story of the life, death, and resurrection of Jesus Christ that launched the church, shaped and sustained its pre-Constantinian life, and to put it to work in today's context with integrity, precision, passion, and cultural relevance. When such authenticity and its inherent hopefulness infect the church, transformation will inevitably happen.

There is a Protestant congregation in Mount Juliet, Tennessee, that in the early 1990s was described by judicatories as being "on life support." Having fifty people in worship on a Sunday was a good day. It had a plethora of committees with the same people belonging to almost all of them. They would meet, talk about how dead everything was, and then do little or nothing. They kept hoping that their proximity to Nashville might eventually generate growth in their community and bring new members and their resources. Long beforehand they had defaulted on their mortgage. The lender kept reducing the interest rate as an incentive to try to jump-start a new series of payments, but the congregation could hardly pay the meager staff it had, much less a mortgage.

In the amazing ways that God works, one of their denominational seminary's brightest, most energetic, articulate, and gospel-centered new graduates was called to lead this congregation. This new pastor had little interest in program development and institutional restructuring. Church administration was not his gift. Instead, he was completely in love with Jesus Christ and the gospel. He was passionate about the church and its identity and calling in the world. In very short order he had gathered a coalition of previous despairing members and invested in them, not with visions of new programs but with the ancient and authentic story of the life, death, and resurrection of Jesus Christ and what it might mean for their congregation. Council meetings were less about committee reports and wringing hands over the lack of funds and were more about spiritual development. Worship was reengineered so that anyone who entered the doors would clearly experience that the congregation was anchored in the richest soil of its sacred identity. Never mind that the congregation could not afford a musician. They sang their hymns *a cappella*, but their worship was authentic.

Within a few months the leadership was looking with new eyes at everything the congregation did. They developed a guiding principle about what they would do and what they would not. "If it has nothing to do with God raising Jesus from the dead," then they would not fool with it. It seemed like overnight this congregation changed. Within a year and a half, worship attendance had doubled and continued to rise. The congregation soon added a unique Sunday-afternoon worship experience called "Talk Back Church." This setting invited people to come to the congregation with whatever questions or concerns they had about God or life. Instead of a sermon, there would be a conversation. Inevitably, what would happen is that instead of questions being answered, the questions would be reframed in light of the life, death, and resurrection of Jesus Christ.

Today that congregation in Mount Juliet is not at all the same as it was in the 1990s. This does not mean that it has not experienced conflict. It has. Dramatic change such as it experienced is going to create conflict. New birth and new life are always a little messy—anybody who has ever been in a delivery room can testify to that. But this congregation—a mainline one at that!—is now seen by many as a powerfully hopeful sign for the future of the church. This is good news, but better news is that the story of this congregation's transformation and vitalization is not unique. In the midst of the cries of despair, troubling conflict, and declining membership in much of the church, there are countless congregations who are experiencing new life, pursuing bold visions, and flourishing.[10]

When authenticity to the church's primal story is the beginning and enduring focus, transformation is going to happen.[11]

Count on it! It will not happen because we, as church leaders, finally came up with the right formula. It will happen because the church's ancient and authentic story itself is a story that *happens* to and thus changes a church community. This is not the work of clever congregational strategists. It is the work of God who raises and breathes new life into the dead. Thus, what follows in this book attends to the particular dynamics of authentic congregational transformation.

Chapter One

Toward Transformation

The treasure of the church is its story. Though the world may change, the church's story and its essential message do not. This whole story, cosmic in nature and implications, incorporates a particular and an essential narrative, the details of which matter, according to the church. This narrative contains certain events that the church receives and claims, by faith, as its own. The creeds of the church articulate essential events of the narrative, but the power of the story is not that it provides some helpful religious information. Rather, its power lies in the fact that the story itself is so true and so compelling that it effects transformation. The story effects transformation because the story confronts us with God. The story grasps us, shakes us, deconstructs in us false pride and self-reliance, and infuses us with God. God both animates the story and comes in the story. Thus, the story includes a narrative, expressed in words, song, and art; and yet, the story is infinitely more than a narrative.

The story comes at us in its clearest essence when we gather in the space where the church worships. When a son or daughter of the church processes to an altar area with acolyte in hand, the candles tell us a promise. No matter how dark the day on which we gather, the light of the story will nevertheless shine and not be overcome. The story enfolds us when we dare to stand or get on our knees with others and confess that we are sinners and then hear that God in great mercy actually forgives us. Our spouse, the co-worker down the hall, or our thirteen year-old daughter might not be ready to truly forgive us, but God does. Even when we cannot forgive ourselves, God forgives. The story comes to us when the scriptures are opened and a preacher dares to use the story to deconstruct our kingdoms and offers us instead the kingdom of God. The most heavily fortified kingdom the story confronts is not a political entity. It is the kingdom of self.

If we are part of a liturgical church, we not only are confronted with the story, we also participate in it. We sing hymns that tell the story. We pray for the whole world and the people of God within the context of the story. We get out our wallets or checkbooks and offer our hard-earned money, not because we need to help pay the church bills but because the story compels us to do so. And if we do not like to sing, or if we want to argue with what the preacher has to say, or if our minds happen to drift during the prayers, God yet confronts us with timeless treasures of the church for which there is no argument or debate. In baptism and in the Eucharist, God comes as God, and that's it! "Child of God, you have been sealed by the Holy Spirit and marked with the cross of Christ forever." "The body of Christ given for you. The blood of Christ shed for you."

The church is not ours. The church is God's. The story is not ours. The story is God's. We are simply stewards of God's story. God's story tells us what God is up to, and God is up to the work of transformation. Transformation happens in the church not because we are so smart or good at what we do. Transformation happens because God is good and is still at work reconciling the world through Christ. After all, the church's claim is not "He *was* risen," but rather, "He *is* risen!"

Transformation is at the heart of what Paul wrote to the church at Rome. "Do not be conformed to this world, but be transformed . . ." (Romans 12:2). Transformation, then, has to do with the change in stories out of which we live, the giving up of certain presuppositions, loyalties, values, and worldviews through the adoption of a different story, or better yet, that different story adopting us! Let me illustrate.

My family and I lived in Iran during the revolution that eventually led to the overthrow of Shah Mohammed Reza Pahlavi. On Christmas Eve 1978, we were gathered around the Christmas tree in our home in Tehran. We were under a mandatory curfew; otherwise we would have worshiped in a local German church. On this night we would "do church" in our home. As nighttime fell, we heard the sounds we had become accustomed to hearing each night. We would hear voices shouting in Farsi from the rooftops: "God is great!" and "Death to the Shah!" and "Death to America!" We would hear the deafening rumble of armored military transports rolling down the street outside our door, taking soldiers to their positions in the city. We would hear machine-gun fire and other eruptions of violence. Inside, my wife, a friend from the United States, and I were singing Christmas carols as loud as we could to keep our small children, whom we held in our arms, from hearing the mayhem outside.

Two stories were being told that night. The story told in the streets was a version of one of the oldest of stories, the story of Cain killing his brother Abel. That story has been reenacted in every age—a tale of the quest for power and the use of force to seize it. It is a story we have never been able to resolve. The second story told that night was the story disclosed in the words of our carols: "Hark! The herald angels sing, 'Glory to the newborn king; peace on earth and mercy mild, God and sinners reconciled'"[1]; "Silent night, holy night! All is calm, all is bright round yon virgin mother and child . . ."[2]

Only one of these stories can be true. Only one will have the last word. The world organizes itself around the story of unresolved human conflict, power struggles, greed, and violence. The church organizes itself around the story of God, who comes to dwell with us, beginning as a defenseless baby, declaring peace and amnesty; being crucified, raised from the dead, and available and accessible to the church as the Living One. The distinction between the two stories is the question of whether sin and death hold the last word or whether God does. Being grasped by one story necessarily requires being in tension with the other.

Today the world's story tells our teenagers that their value comes from looks, the "right clothes," sex appeal, popularity, and accomplishments. The church's story tells them they are inherently valuable just as they are. The world's story tells us to take control of our lives and eliminate uncertainty. The church's story calls us to trust in the God who raised Jesus from the dead, and to accept that living in ambiguity is not only healthy—it is also unavoidable! The world's story tells us that personal failure is greatly to be feared. The church's story lifts up Jesus Christ crucified as one rejected by all. The world tells us that we have only limited resources. The church's story, declaring that there is enough for all, calls us to reorder our lives so that others might live. The church's story will always be in tension with the world's.

One of the traps of world-oriented thinking is the belief that *we have to do something* to make transformation happen. Thus, many search for the next results-guaranteed program or strategy. Others may attempt to replicate a success story at another congregation, as if congregational success can be bottled and sold. Yet, the rich soil of the church makes it clear that transformation is God's work. Transformation, then, does not inherently happen through tactics, new programs, or church-growth strategies. It happens through the church digging deep into the very theological substance of its life as the body of Christ in the world and drawing from that rich soil in such ways that people cannot help but have their lives reoriented. The substance that creates transformation is never in the tactics. It's always in the soil.

A read of the whole Bible makes it clear that God is always the author of transformation. In a number of central biblical stories, there is a consistently predictable pattern in which transformation is the outcome. In his book *Biblical Perspectives on Evangelism*, biblical scholar Walter Brueggemann describes this pattern as a threefold "drama."[3] The pattern begins with God winning a victory over something of life-threatening importance to us—creation out of chaos, deliverance from slavery, and raising Jesus from the dead, for example. That victory is then announced, whether it is Miriam taking her tambourine in her hand and going out dancing and singing with the women her victory song (Exodus 15:20-21), Mary Magdalene announcing to the disciples that she has seen the risen Lord (John 20:18), or Peter standing up and addressing the crowd on the Day of Pentecost with the announcement that God has raised up the crucified Jesus and made him Lord and Messiah of all (Acts 2:32-26). Those who then experience the announcement of the victory cannot remain neutral. They cannot walk away, simply saying, "Well, that was nice," or, "That was interesting," and go back to resuming their lives as before. The announcement comes as such astonishingly good news that they are compelled to reorder everything about their lives and reorient their relationship to the world in light of what they have experienced. The three thousand who were baptized on the Day of Pentecost (Acts 2:41) and their subsequent life together (Acts 2:42-47) represents such a reorientation. Biblically speaking, a metamorphosis (see Romans 12:2) has occurred.

Transformation: Our Needs Versus God's Needs

Judaism, Islam, and the church all agree on two things: God exists, and we are not God! In a context of consumer relationships with the church, this basic understanding of these great monotheistic religions often gets flip-flopped. Rather than our being subjected to the lordship of God, we want to put God at our service. This notion of coercing God to support our own agendas is very Constantinian. It also means, in the language of today, that the church and its God exist to meet consumer needs. Such a consumer relationship cannot help but work to trivialize God.

For sure the church, because of the power and substance of its story, includes multitudes of people who have been grasped by the gospel, hold God in great awe, are being theologically transported on a journey of transformation, and yet maintain a consumer orientation. The difference in this form of consumerism and the form that trivializes God is that this form of consumerism is about discernment. Consumers of this type do not want to be treated as consumers. They want to be grasped by

Biblical Transformation

The root of the biblical Greek word that Paul uses in Romans 12:2, and which the editors of the *New Revised Standard Version* of the Bible translated "transformed," is *metamorphomai*, from which we get the word *metamorphosis*. In the New Testament, it is used only four times. In addition to Romans 12:2, it is used in the story of Jesus being "transfigured" on the mountain (cf. Mark 9:2 and Matthew 17:2), and in 2 Corinthians 3:18. In this last use, Paul argues that as the church beholds the glory of the Lord, the church is ". . . being transformed into the same image from one degree of glory to another . . ." "Glory" here means to reflect Christ as a mirror reflects an image.

Metamorphosis, as understood by the Greek root and as understood in our language today, means more than a cosmetic change. It is a complete structural change. A metamorphic rock is a rock that has been changed, due to heat or pressure, from one substance to another. Its basic building blocks—its atoms—are the same, but its molecular structure is different. Thus, a diamond is the result of the metamorphosis of coal. Petroleum is the result of the metamorphosis of dead organic matter. A piece of coal is not a diamond. A collection of rotting plants and animal carcasses is not petroleum. It takes transformation, wrought by forces acting upon them, to become that which is completely new.

Biblical transformation then means a complete change, brought about by the activity of God, in which people become different from what they were before— not cosmetically different but really different. As Paul writes in 2 Corinthians 5:16-17, transformation means "we regard no one from a human point of view; . . . so if anyone is in Christ, there is a new creation: everything old has passed away; see, everything has become new."

authenticity and can sense it when it exists. They simply will not settle for less. They will not settle for entertainment masquerading as worship. They will not settle for self-improvement sermons as substitutes for proclamation that works to put our religious schemes and projects to death and leave us with only God on whom to rely. They have been immersed in the deep rich soil of the ancient and authentic story of the church, and they will not settle for artificial substitutes.

Such was the case with a family described to me by another pastor while we were at a church conference. The family had recently moved to his area, joined his church, and after a few months left. They took the trouble to inform him that the reason that they were leaving was that they did not feel challenged enough. In this instance the issue had to do with financial stewardship. They wanted a church that demanded more of them as they reoriented their lives in light of the gospel. It was not that they simply wanted the church to ask them for more money. What they wanted was the church's story to so infect them that they would be compelled to be more generous and to live on less. They had been on a path toward increased giving with their previous congregation and in their move to another church, the spiritual force driving that movement had atrophied. Wouldn't all pastors love to have an abundance of families like this one in our congregations?

The vast form of consumerism the church encounters is quite different from the situation with this family that demanded substance. This more common consumerism is not seeking transformation; it has an agenda of other personal needs: "Pay attention to me! Fix my marriage. Fix my teenager. Support my personal political beliefs and social agenda. Help God to bless my efforts to become richer. Affirm my lifestyle. Don't challenge it. And when I come into worship after an especially rough week, give me a good uplifting experience." This personal agenda is not new. It is as old as the conversation in the Garden of Eden between the talking snake and the first humans. The first expression of sin is our rejection of the notion that we are not God or at least cannot be like God. We are to be served!

Again, the church does not belong to us. The church is God's. The church is God's social strategy for the world. God loves the whole world. God's need is that the whole world experience abundant life—abundant life as defined by God and not the world. Transformation happens when people are so grasped by God's agenda that they begin to abandon their own needs and agenda and they discover this change in orientation as exceedingly great news. Their experience of transformation restructures their own perceived needs and questions. They see themselves differently. They see the world differently. They see the church differently. Instead of existing in relationship to the church as a consumer, they find themselves to be at home as citizens of the church and its story of God reconciling the world through Christ. They begin a reordering of their lives, which continues as they are drawn deeper into the richness of the story. As transformation continues, they see more clearly what the world cannot see, dream what the world cannot dream, and work for what the world cannot work, all because God, through God's church, has grasped them.

On a Tuesday after a recent Holy Week, Paul, one of our pastoral interns, reflected in a small group on an experience he had the previous week. Paul had made a run to the grocery store after our Good Friday worship. While standing in the checkout line he noticed the cover of one of the magazines in the display rack, which featured a very attractive teenage girl. She was well endowed, thin, physically fit, and scantily clad. On the cover were these words: "You can have a body just like this one!" Paul said that after being immersed in the church's story in the intensive way that Holy Week immerses us and experiencing how it is that Jesus Christ's death was God's affirmation of the infinite worth of all human beings, this encounter with the magazine's cover message angered him. The cover was from a world that exists in opposition to the church. As the cover begged to invite him into the false promise it offered, he said that he was carrying in his soul an image proffered in our worship center that night: the accusers pointing their fingers at Jesus. Paul worked among our high school youth, which included a particular young lady whose genetic make-up meant that she would always be heavy. She regularly had to endure some dehumanizing bullying at school, and Paul experienced the magazine as a cultural statement of the world pointing its finger at this girl. Outside the church, the world saw a fat teenager who probably had little going for her. Inside the church she had infinite worth and was a leader among our youth. Paul's eyes on that night became indicative of the new eyes given with transformation. The church is the contrast society in which the transformed make their home.

Transformation and Adaptation

The main task before the church in this time of cultural transition, confusion, and opportunity is the recovery of its authentic story. That includes the creation of a congregational culture whose self-understanding and ethos emerge from the DNA of its story. Perhaps the insightful work of leadership expert Ronald Heifetz will be helpful here. The basic theory that Heifetz introduces in his book *Leadership without Easy Answers,* and further develops in a sequel (*Leadership on the Line,* coauthored with his Harvard colleague Marty Linsky), is the proposal that leadership often fails because it inadvertently offers "technical" solutions to situations that beg for "adaptive" leadership.[4] Both books convincingly make the case that leading people through technical change is something much more easily done than leading people through adaptive change. Technical leadership does not really seek transformation among those it serves. Technical solutions simply have the leadership doing something for those it serves. Those who are served only need to accept—not adapt to—the technical change. Adaptive leadership, on the other hand, can be quite perilous. Adaptive leadership calls upon people to give up certain ways of thinking, perhaps some loyalties, and certain assumptions with which they participate in the world. Adaptive leadership calls upon people to change collectively, giving up one paradigm or story and owning another paradigm or story. Galileo did that at great peril, as well as another leader who dared to institute radical social change in America, Martin Luther King Jr.

A helpful illustration might be our government's handling of the September 11, 2001 event, which one could fairly conclude was an almost completely technical response.[5]Attention was paid to beefing up homeland security, raising the level of screening at our airports, and sending troops into Afghanistan. As I was envisioning this book, the United States launched its war against Iraq. Our troops moved quickly into Baghdad, destroyed the governing regime's hold on the people, and declared victory, an utterly technical approach to the threat of terrorism.

The reality of international terrorism is something that begs for adaptive leadership. It raises all kinds of questions: What are situations that have led to terrorism? Are any of our policies fostering such situations? Is there anything we need to do to change global opinions toward us? Why do some hate us? How do we keep our ideals and values as a nation and at the same time positively participate in a world that has given birth to terrorism? No doubt, these are very difficult and dangerous questions. Venturing into serious conversation and naming some brutal truths are not done without great peril. On the other hand, if there is not some sort of transformation of our global community and in people's consciousness away from terrorism, all the technical approaches in the world will not be enough.

All the technical approaches are not enough because terrorism itself is a technical approach—an inhumane tactic taken by those who find difficulty in utilizing adaptive approaches to address their perceived dilemma in today's world. The apparent conundrum of dealing with terrorism is complicated by perhaps our own struggle to recognize terrorism as simply a tactic. Terrorism by intent creates a climate of fear, and fear itself fuels quick-fix political motives. That this discussion has focused, as an example, on our post-9/11 response is not to pick on one particular political party. Neither political party has seemed especially adept at embracing and entering into the more adaptive and albeit risky approaches.

The truth—and my larger point—is that we Americans excel at technical solutions. Effective adaptive leadership is another thing. Again, to draw from our global situation, witness the stubborn difficulty in bringing about a new political system in Iraq. As of the writing of this book, the situation in Iraq is still quite unstable. The technical victory declared was one thing. Bringing about a massive adaptation among the Iraqi people—an adaptation to which they will give themselves—is another.

Grasping the differences between technical and adaptive approaches is also important for the church and the work of transformation. Transformation is an adaptive movement requiring intentional adaptive leadership. The adaptation is the giving up of one set of loyalties, priorities, self-understandings, attitudes, and worldviews and claiming another set because one has been grasped by the church's story. This is not to say that technical approaches do not belong in the church. My goodness, solid technical approaches are essential to the daily and long-term life of any congregation today. A pastor and a congregational staff are constantly presented with issues that need technical solutions, whether it is how to handle parking on Easter Sunday, whether to print the worship bulletins on a church photocopier or through the services of a printing company, or the technical decision to relocate the entire facilities to a new location for missional reasons. In the case of the latter, a technical move to a new campus will of course require enormous adaptive leadership savvy to empower a congregation for the emotional, transitional, and other issues such a move would require. The point here is that much related to the transformation of the church today requires appropriate technical decisions that must be followed with skilled adaptive leadership.

The challenge the church faces is that technical approaches to ministry are too often substitutes for transformation. Look at most of the initiatives and strategies for reform that are at work in the church today. This is not to say that they do not have some usefulness, but they are almost overwhelmingly some sort of technical solution. With all due respect to the genuineness of those who align with the church-growth movement and with appreciation for the role that movement has played as a catalyst for change and church renewal, the entire movement is essentially technical in approach. A great gift that ELCA pastor Mark Olson gave to the church before his death in 2003 is his book *Moving beyond Church Growth.*[6] In the opening chapter, Olson takes ten ways of thinking that are imbedded in the modern worldview and connects them to the tenets of the church-growth movement.[7] It is important to remember that the modern world mind-set believed that every problem could be broken down into identifiable parts, and every problem required rational thinking and rational solutions. So Olson examines the church-growth movement—its orientation toward human ingenuity, the demystification of God, the specialization of ministry, mechanistic thinking, its marketing strategies, its orientation to meeting people's needs, and more—and names the approaches modern. Heifetz would call them technical.

Erwin McManus, lead pastor of Mosaic, a multicultural congregation in Los Angeles, uses a helpful term, "cultural architecture," to describe what a congregation does with its worship, environment, and words to tell a story that creates and brings to life a certain cultural ethos and a congregation's understanding of itself.[8] Cultural architecture is intentional and focused. It sets up how God goes to work on a congregation, effecting an adaptive transformation when God's story is consistently told through the church's liturgy[9] with clarity and precision. It focuses not on technical strategies but focuses on the richness of the soil that grounds the church and out of which the church's cultural architecture emerges.

I am convinced that much of the church's frustration and confusion today is due to its being stuck in technical approaches in a time that demands adaptive leadership. We live in a new day. Leadership approaches that worked in the previous era will not work in this post-Constantinian and postmodern era. They also will not work in an era in which the relevancy of denominationalism and its forms of church polity are under question. I believe that pastors suffer from burnout and depression, not because they are poor at self-care, but because they are stuck in systems that no longer work. They are exhausted from one technical approach after another. They know deep down inside that something is inherently wrong. I believe that non-paid congregational leaders likewise suffer from frustration and burnout because of attending to an exhausting technical agenda, and they too sense that something is wrong. Bishops and judicatory executives are troubled and confused, many confessing that they spend too much of their time immersed in the pathologies of congregations and pastors because they hold positions in church bodies that are so entrenched in institutionalism and its technical approach to virtually everything that they cannot adapt to this new day. So they live in constant tension. Perhaps the instances these days of bishops who try to throw their ecclesiastical weight around are born out of anxious reactivity to a world that no longer wants to take them seriously. Perhaps they sense that their technical capital is exhausted.

I believe that seminary students look with anxiety toward the time when they will enter into service in the church because they intuitively know that much of what they learned in their field education is technical in approach and will be insufficient to lead a church in today's world. I believe that many congregations are angry with their pastors, that pastors are angry with their bishops, and bishops, pastors, and congregations are all angry with the seminaries because there is no technical solution to the confusion the church faces over its identity and calling and the pain and tension that confusion causes.

The church to which Jesus calls us to enter is a wholly adaptive movement. It is a movement that turns from taking clues on how to live from a world that has been declared dead and turns to the gospel of Jesus Christ as the true and living story that reorders our lives. Without being overly simplistic, it means to just be the church. The first adaptive movement might be the realization that Jesus indeed did not come to meet our needs. Jesus came and God birthed the church to meet God's needs by raising up a community that exists as a sign or witness to God's redemptive activity in the world. Certainly God's needs include that we "might have life and have it abundantly" (John 10:10). But the movement to this life is adaptive, losing life—losing our schemes, deals, causes, and whatever else the world tells us we must have in order for our lives to be significant and meaningful—and finding it by walking in a new and true story. This movement is not easy. The Jesus who calls us into this movement did not first do so without great peril. It cost him his life, but as Joey Sherman, a young man in my congregation wrote, "He would not stay dead because he loves us."[10]

Advance Scouts for an Emerging Church

The central thesis of this book—the relationship between authenticity to the church's primal story and true transformation—is not just a theory, nor is it nostalgia or a fascination with a long-ago church in a long-ago and foreign culture. Rather, it is a hope-filled proposition, grounded in the reality of the existence of vital congregations that provide substance for the renewal of the church in North America. They exist as wonderful challenges to the notion that the North American church, especially its mainline expressions, has seen its best days. They suggest that this postmodern, post-Christendom, and secular age in which we are living actually could be one of the most exciting times to be the church.

Simply stated, vital congregations are congregations that are alive. They get their life not from their latest strategies but from their stubborn refusal to play on Astroturf. They are solidly anchored and get their life from the rich soil of the church's ancient and authentic story. These vital congregations exist in virtually every setting, come in all sizes, and do not belong to just one way of being the church.

From the moment that one enters into the life of one of these many vital congregations, one senses a positive and healthy spirit. There is the clear sense that the people gathered are caught up in something that matters, and whatever it is that matters has found great traction in their lives. These congregations are real, yet imaginative. They are not afraid to address the depths of the human condition and enter into the darkest arenas of human pain and suffering. At the same time, these congregations seem to exhibit unshakable hopefulness, thankfulness, and joy about life itself and the future. These congregations know how to cry together and laugh together.

These congregations can also be expected to exhibit great courage. They are not afraid of change. They know from where their strength comes. When presented with a challenge—whether it is a project that is going to require lots of resources, the reordering of their life together in order to reach more people, or restructuring staff for missional purposes—they rise up to meet the challenge. They are also places of creative conflict. Conflict is inevitable in communities where passions run deep about the very life of the community and its clarity of purpose. Yet, as places where creative conflict is welcomed, these congregations simultaneously are places of healing. One can expect them to be filled with lots of grace. Vital congregations are also resilient. They have enormous capacities to weather adversity.

Such a weathering capacity in my own congregation was put to the test beginning on April 20, 1999 with the Columbine High School shootings. We were what the disaster response experts named a "ground-zero congregation." When we were shaken to our core with this massacre of our own sons and daughters, and when we collectively seemed to suffer from post-traumatic stress syndrome, the disaster response experts kept telling us that healthy systems are resilient. Thankfully, the experts were right.

Another aspect of the resiliency aspect is worth mentioning here. Following the shootings, disaster-response experts came to our community and revealed some sobering data. Based upon their research, it would be expected that all the pastors and ground-zero caregivers would have moved on from the community within two years after the shootings.[11] Almost all mainline "ground-zero" congregations associated with the Columbine event fulfilled this expectation. My congregation and I did not. We went against the trend.

The fifth anniversary of the Columbine High School shootings gave cause for one person interested in this predictable effect on pastors and caregivers to examine my congregation to try to discern why we did not fit the pattern.[12] What she discovered was that our resiliency was not related to *emotional* health per se but to *theological* health. We were deeply anchored in the story of Jesus Christ crucified and risen, believed it to be true, and richly used the core texts and appropriated the ancient rituals of the church in ways that dealt authentically with the deathly reality of the shootings and at the same time the unshakable promise and hope of the Christian gospel. Perhaps Erwin McManus would propose that an authentic cultural architecture had been so birthed and intentionally nurtured in our congregation that, of course, it would weather the storms of Columbine. This is not to suggest that other congregations in our immediate area, who did not fare so well, were somehow theologically flawed or emotionally unhealthy. It does, however, disclose a theologically based resiliency in our setting.

Health Indicators

Although vital congregations demonstrate great diversity in how their lives are ordered and what their flagship ministries might be, some consistency can be noted regarding particular statistical markers that identify these congregations. Just as blood-pressure measurements, cholesterol levels, and the readings of other important body chemistries are indicators of personal health, congregations also have some relative health indicators. I identify four indicators that are easily measurable and which I have found useful in suggesting the presence of authentic vitality. The first is *an overall upward trend in average weekly worship attendance.* This is a trend over time. Every congregation will experience periodic dips and plateaus, as well as some real obstacles to growth that have nothing to do with a congregation's authenticity or vitality. Sometimes a community experiences decline in its population. Sometimes physical limitations—size of facilities and parking—affect growth. Sometimes a congregation goes through a period when it needs to reinvent how it is organized to pursue its mission. Sometimes churches undergo painful adaptive transitions as the role and relationship of pastors and staff to the congregation must necessarily shift because a way of being that worked when the congregation was one size no longer works as the congregation has grown to a different size. Sometimes when a congregation's culture changes or its missional foci are aligned differently people leave. The point here is not to suggest that a vital congregation has to demonstrate consistent annual growth, but the truth is that healthy systems grow. Just ask any gardener. The discussion here is also not to suggest that bigger is better. The point is that healthy systems do indeed generally grow.

The second factor is *the percentage of membership that worships weekly*. Healthy systems have a strong gravitational pull toward its life together and particularly toward worship. Like a tree whose roots search and reach down into the richest soil, people are simply drawn into authentic worship to soak up its life-giving power. My experience is that vital congregations, as described in the previous paragraphs, usually also claim a worship-to-membership ratio of 40 percent or higher. That is close to double the national mainline Protestant average and assumes that the congregation's membership rolls are quite clean. One should be cautious about making this a hard and fast rule, however. Some congregations may have a high percentage of shut-ins on their rolls or some other set of circumstances that significantly affect this marker. On the other hand, lacking any special circumstances, a ratio below 40 percent would suggest that there is some adaptive work to do. Some congregations actually exhibit weekly worship attendance that exceeds their membership. Such is the case of a Lutheran congregation in Damascus, Maryland, and a nondenominational congregation in Lakewood, Colorado. There are many more.

The third indicator of health is *the average giving of each household expressed as a percentage of household income*. Because money and wealth are held at idolatrous levels in our culture, one's wallet is usually the last aspect of one's life to be converted. Vital congregations exhibit an overall upward trend over time in the percentage of the income their households give. Moreover, vital congregations are seemingly more immune to the effects of economic downturns and may even experience higher levels of giving in such times.

The last indicator is *the percentage of a congregation's overall spending plan (i.e., budget) that is given for mission and ministries beyond its doors.* Again, the indicator is an overall increasing trend over time. Congregations who believe that they are caught up in something that matters give themselves to the world rather than imploding by an overly inward focus. A wise mentor of mine once said, "Whenever you hear a congregation saying, 'We need to first take care of our own,' that is a sign of a congregation who is dying."

There are certainly other factors that also suggest vitality. These four are not infallible or inerrant, and a word of caution is necessary here. Lest anyone believe that a congregation cannot be vital without showing growth in all these areas, sometimes economic conditions and population trends are so significantly adverse that such growth is quite difficult. Taken together, however, they do seemingly paint a picture of relative health for most settings. In vital congregations, people see themselves less as "belonging to a church" and are more caught up in the notion that they "are the church."

A Different Cultural Architecture

Vital congregations that are grounded in the church's ancient and authentic story have a self-understanding that distinguishes them from congregations whose self-understanding is conflicted, confused, obfuscated, and perhaps unknowingly shallow. They have a different cultural architecture about the way they define themselves and the ways their lives are ordered. They own their identity and calling with clarity and precision. Rather than playing on Astroturf they live out of the good soil. Rather than focusing on technical approaches they work towards adaptive transformation. They are not consumer driven. They are God driven.

Table 1 on the following page introduces some building blocks of a cultural architecture that is intentional about the formation of an authentic transformational church. These are theological and ecclesiological building blocks. They are not strategies. The sixth chapter of this book, "Intentional Congregational Architecture," will propose a fuller matrix of the building blocks.

Table 1
Cultural Architecture for an Authentic Transformational Church

FROM	TO
• The church inherited from Constantine	• Authentic
• Technical in Approach	• Adaptive Transformation
• Consumer-driven	• God-driven

The Church

• Institution to which people might belong	• A movement of people "in Christ"
• Offers deals for salvation	• Exists as a witness to the new reality and its promised future as disclosed in the ancient and authentic story of the life, death and resurrection of Jesus Christ
• Takes up causes that benefit the community and world	
• Serves as a chaplain offering spiritual services and programs	• A contrast community

The Meaning of Membership

• Membership	• Partnership and ownership
• Could be necessary for salvation	• Membership itself is a witness to the new reality and the promised future
• Fitting God into "my" story	• Surrenders self to God's story
• Insures having "my" needs met	• Is called to meet God's needs

The Role of the Pastors and Staff

• Pastors and staff serve as chaplains to meet needs	• Pastors and staff serve as stewards of the church's story
• Dispensers of programs and service	• They provide transformational, adaptive servant-leadership
• They "run" the church	• They build up and equip all to own the church's identity and calling
• Members of the "clergy club" have higher authority and power than "the laity"	• They bow down to their calling and lift others up to fulfill the mission

Baptism

• A deal to escape damnation	• Initiation into the church as a contrast community
• One of the services the church offers	• Confers identity and calling

These first ones are introduced here to give a partial picture of the kind of adaptive moves that will be needed for the deconstruction of a congregation stuck in a Constantinian hangover and the reconstruction of the authentic church.

Baptism is included in this initial table because the culture's grasp of baptism is an indicator of just how lost the idea of the church as a contrast society is from the culture's consciousness. Nonmembers who approach the church inquiring about baptism for their child are almost invariably immersed in the technical aspects of baptism. For sure, because of the doctrine of some traditions, there are those who understand baptism as necessary for salvation (or at least want to hedge against any chance that it might be!). For this reason, many come to the church just wanting to get their kid "done." Never mind that baptism itself is an adaptive ritual, mediating a change in paradigms and initiating a life in Christ through the church. "Just-getting-the-deal-done" thinking co-opts it into a technical event. Others come tied up in other technicalities: "Can we take pictures?" "Will you carry her down aisle like you did with that other baby? That was so cute!" "Can we play a CD of this song? It is very touching." "Do we really have to be members ourselves?" Anybody who thinks that these technical questions are not to be taken seriously has never encountered the intensity with which our consumer culture expects the church to service their needs.

Church Architecture and Transformation

I earlier stated that I intend for this book to be hopeful. I share the following story because it is one sign among countless manifestations of amazing transformation taking place in vital congregations everywhere. It is truly God's story of God at work in the world. In February 2001, I was privileged to journey to Haiti with a team from our congregation. The journey was a search for intentional mission. It was not the search for a cause. This mission trip emerged out of a long, prayerful, and study-driven congregational process in which the congregation clarified its own identity and calling in the world. This process produced a new vision statement, which affirmed the congregation's essential calling to be an authentic witness to the life, death, and resurrection of Jesus Christ. It clearly stated that Jesus Christ and his sacred story would be the guide for the congregation's every thought, word, or action. Worship was named as the main expression of the congregation's calling, deserving of our highest and best attention, and as the core architect and source of empowerment for the rest of the congregation's witness. A number of specific foci were named as expressions of our witness as the body of Christ in and for the world. These foci were not a list of technical strategies to employ. Rather, they specified the nature of the witness the congregation believed God was calling it to exhibit. One of the foci said that the congregation would stand with the poor, the powerless, and the disenfranchised with the compassion of Christ that has no limits or boundaries.[13]

Understand that the very nature of the guiding statements that emerged from the congregational process was a result of the congregation already being deeply immersed in the rich soil of the church's ancient and authentic story. This immersion began with the launching of this congregation. Like the new seminary graduate who was called to the congregation in Mt. Juliet, Tennessee, the congregation's mission developer and first pastor was not passionate about church administration and three- and four-point strategies. He was passionate about Jesus, the gospel, and the mission of the church. Those who first gathered as a new congregation were infected with his passion. They ultimately owned it and shared it.

Being drawn into the passion that goes back to the birth of this congregation and being faithful to the congregation's commitment to stand with the poor, this team went to Haiti. If the congregation was truly going to stand with the poor, it *had* to go to Haiti. This is not to devalue the many compassionate efforts the congregation undertakes in the Denver community, but Haiti is the poorest country in the entire Western hemisphere. There is one level of being poor, and then there is Haiti poor.

Only God could have imagined what would develop from that first initial trip. Within the year and after more trips, the Haitian Timoun Foundation was formed. "Timoun" in Haitian

Creole means "little ones." The foundation's mission is to support Christian-based agencies in Haiti who hold great potential to change the lives of children there. On the surface, this initiative provides many of the adventures to which many postmoderns are attracted: international travel, experiences of a different culture, opportunities for hands-on ministry experiences, and feelings of being engaged in something that matters. But those who are in the center of this initiative and its development bear in their lives and witness more than just a desire to do something "meaningful" that makes them "feel good."

Spending time with these people discloses that they are seized by something much more profound, the crucified and living Christ and his church. They are people who have literally been immersed in the church's story and stay immersed. They are leading the charge for this mission in Haiti because they have been seized by a gospel that has called them. One of the principal leaders is a highly gifted woman who has been so transformed by the church's authenticity that she left her high-powered, six-figure career with a major syndicated radio company to give herself more fully to the church. She sings in the choir, shepherds our middle-school kids, and gives herself to the Haiti initiative. Another principal is a lifelong child of the church and a former nurse who gives herself to this initiative while also being a foster parent to battered kids in our community. Another principal is a former nutritionist who no longer works at a paying job and gives herself to the church primarily through this initiative. There is also a paramedic and a music therapist, both having professional gifts that are quite useful in Haiti, especially among diseased and mentally or physically challenged children.

Here are some of the results (which I hesitantly share with you, not wanting to be accused of flaunting some "success" story; this is God's success story): primarily due to the Haiti initiative, in 2002 the total gifts of the congregation to mission beyond its doors increased by 62 percent. This increase happened during a major economic recession and in the midst of a major building project. The initiative hopes to be investing, by the end of this decade, over a $1,000,000 a year in Haiti, and it seems that it is well on its way to getting there. The initiative has caught the attention and support of other congregations, some far away from Littleton, Colorado.

Do you have any idea what a $1,000,000 a year might do in Haiti? As I previously mentioned, it is the poorest country in the Western hemisphere: the average per capita income is around $250 per year. As of the writing of this book, the foundation's investment in Haiti is having a direct impact on over 1,300 kids. For many, the investment means the difference in having a bed in which to sleep and food to eat. After all, our Lord does expect such things from us. "I was hungry and you fed me, naked and you clothed me" (Matthew 25:35-36). But perhaps more importantly, the investment in Haiti means that children are now being given an alternative future. Children who heretofore had no hope of getting an education or learning job skills and who would have to depend upon charity for the rest of their lives have a shot at not only being able to carve out a better life for themselves but also being able to contribute to the positive development of Haiti itself.

Imagine what could happen to the North American church if everybody decided to get together and call a moratorium on three-, five-, and ten-year strategic plans. Imagine what might happen if instead of focusing on program development the church first focused on theological renewal and the rekindling of a first-century passion? What if the church became very intentional about stripping away all its superficiality and market-driven initiatives and played only in the rich soil? Could it be possible that such renewal would take place that the North American church would be accused of the same charge leveled at the infant church? These are the people "who have been turning the world upside down" (Acts 17:6).

Chapter Two

A Searching Culture from the Kingdom of Self

On a beautiful fall Sunday against the backdrop of the Front Range of the Rockies, I was standing on our church grounds with a cup of coffee in my hand. Worship had ended and people were gathered in our grassy courtyard area, engaged in conversation with one another before heading off to their next activity. A very attractive couple, whom I estimate to have been in their late thirties or early forties, approached me. They introduced themselves and introduced their two elementary-school-aged children. They were first-time visitors. Though they were dressed in the casual attire that is usual for churchgoers in our western suburban culture, their impeccable outward appearance suggested that they were economically affluent. After some exchange of niceties, I asked a question I frequently ask of first-time visitors, "What brought you to Abiding Hope?" They were both very talkative. I quickly learned that they both were well educated, having attended prestigious undergraduate and graduate-level professional schools. They both held "great" jobs and lived in a very upscale development. They were not native Coloradans but had moved here from Minnesota a few years earlier. Their kids were enrolled in a private school and were involved in many activities. They told me that their lives were "great" and that they were "happy." Their reason for coming on this Sunday morning, however, was because they were sensing that "something was missing" and were seeking a connection to a "spiritual community" that would be "the icing on the cake" for their otherwise wonderful lives.

I would have liked to have explored more of what they were trying to say to me by the "icing on the cake" expression. Through the little exchange we were able to have in that setting they wanted me to know that they had everything that they needed in this world—prestigious degrees, well-paying jobs, good health, a fine home, children who would no doubt be successful, and the many other rewards that come with fruitfully pursuing the American Dream—but one aspect of their lives, the spiritual aspect, was not in place. They came to worship a few more times, then I never saw them again. I do not know if they found another congregation, moved away, or simply gave up their search for their "icing on the cake."

Whatever their motivation for being in worship with us for a few times and whatever their reason for not returning, one thing is clear: they entered into the doors of our congregation as consumers. They had needs to be met, and they were searching. Whatever the reason, our congregation did not meet their needs. Maybe they were seeking something a little less chaotic. Maybe they had a bad experience with somebody—maybe with me! I am not picking on this couple as being especially spiritually impoverished; rather, I offer this illustration as a launching pad for a discussion on my experience with postmoderns who speak in the "success" language I often hear and who yet feel spiritually confused, troubled, or incomplete.

A conundrum in the postmodern experience is that postmoderns—that is, those who live out of a postmodern worldview—are aware, at least subconsciously, that the modern world has collapsed, taking down with it religious assumptions out of which they once lived, and at the same time, they sense that clear replacements are not yet accessible to them. Because many norms of the modern world have been displaced, postmoderns are generally a spiritually seeking and searching group. Postmoderns and the search for worldly success do not necessarily go hand in hand, but suburban postmoderns can speak in success language of the day, while at the same time being aware of their spiritual incompleteness. (However, one should avoid the assumption that spiritual incompleteness must necessarily be a byproduct of "success"—it's not. The point here is that the pursuit of "success" in terms of our world today is often, if not likely, at the expense of spiritual wellness and wholeness.)[1]

My assumption in this encounter with the couple is that their comment about "icing on the cake" most likely speaks to some deeper yearning that is more than simply "icing on the cake," that is, some form of bonus to an otherwise complete and satisfying life. Having all that one desires in terms of accomplishments, appearances, status, wealth, and lifestyle still leaves people wanting at a level that even "icing on the cake" cannot satisfy. Often people are unable to express just how conflicted or troubled their souls are. This is not to say that folks are deliberately disingenuous. The pursuit of the American Dream is well embedded as a primal cultural script of our world. It promises the "good life" to those who successfully pursue it. At the same time, people who do pursue the American Dream are often blinded or in denial to the realities of the depth of their own human predicament or dilemma. Because of the cultural confusion over the identity and calling of the church, people often then approach the church seeking to address "that something that is missing." People often come to worship seeking God's blessings on their lifestyles, thinking that experiencing some expression of reassuring affirmation might be enough to quell their sense of incompleteness or confusion. Or they might come thinking that the addition of some spiritual component to their lives, not unlike membership in a health club, might be enough to make them whole. Using the language of Ronald Heifetz, they are seeking a purely "technical" solution for "that something that is missing." The very idea that nothing short of a complete reorientation of their lives—reframing everything in the light of a sacred story—might serve to address their dilemma would not likely be in their consciousness. Should such an idea creep into their minds, it would be quickly dismissed as an unacceptable thought. Being put to death in order to be raised to new life is anything but simply "icing on the cake."

Often searchers and "faith shoppers" last only a few Sundays in our congregations because either they fail to hear what they want to hear or what they hear is just too much, perhaps requiring an adaptive journey they are not willing to make. They are not the first to walk away from the church or from Jesus and his claims. There was the rich young man in Mark 10:17-22 who approached Jesus with a technical question about what he needed to do in order "to inherit eternal life." After all, he had everything he thought he needed—wealth plus a track record of keeping all the commandments. In his religious context, this meant that he did everything right. Surely Jesus would be so impressed with his resumé that he would simply be praised by Jesus. The worst case would be that Jesus would point out some minor little adjustment or oversight to which he could easily attend. Instead, Jesus called him to a complete reorientation of his life. Speaking in the rhetoric of today's world, he "rattled his paradigm." He told him to get rid of everything that gave him his identity and which he held to be of ultimate importance. "Sell what you have and give it to the poor" and "follow me." The rich young man could not do that. He left Jesus "grieving."

The Kingdom of Self

Human beings are unlike all other living species. The scriptures claim that we are created "in the image of God" (cf. Genesis 1). The psalmist writes about how wonderful it is that we are made just "a little lower than God" (Psalm 8). The biblical theme for the high status of our rank in the creative order is our call to have "dominion" (cf. Genesis 1 and Psalm 8 again) over the rest of creation. The biblical nuance of "dominion" is that we serve as agents for God. We are stewards of what belongs to God. God is in charge. We work for God. We answer to God. The human grasp of "dominion," on the other hand, means that *we* are in charge! This tension of just *who* is in charge is at the center of the entire biblical narrative. Taken as a whole, the biblical story exposes human sin and rebellion against God and at the same time proclaims God's actions to restore all of creation to a rightful relationship with God.

The kingdom of self is indeed a heavily fortified kingdom. All of human history bears witness to the basic orientation of human beings to first look out for "number one." In America, however, the value of the kingdom of self seemingly rises to another level. Books that focus on looking out for number one, taking control of one's life, and getting what one wants out of life are usually on someone's best-seller list. Seminars that promise to unlock the vast potential of personal power sell lots of tickets. Our culture's highly litigious climate, including an epidemic of frivolous law suits, mean that the kingdom of self is not going to be pushed around. The self is not only going to get what it deserves. The self is also going to go after whatever it can. The value of the kingdom of self is deep within our cultural soul.

American Individualism

Grasping the American value of autonomy and the unique value of the self is critically important if we are to understand the American cultural values in which the church lives. In 1985, Berkeley professor Robert Bellah and certain of his colleagues published their landmark book *Habits of the Heart: Individualism and Commitment in American Life.*[2] Bellah and his colleagues looked deep into the philosophical, literary, and psychological forces that have shaped American character and offered up "individualism" as the primary American cultural value. Note the word *primary* here.

In its essence, individualism means that "I am in charge. I decide what is good for me and what is not. I make my own choices. I have a right to pursue my own needs and my own dreams. I choose my own values. And I have the right to change my values if I so choose, if such a change is in my best interest. Though some laws are necessary to protect the public and to protect us from each other, apart from breaking the law, I can do whatever I want because my needs matter. And in some cases, I am even justified in breaking the law."

Individualism does not mean that we Americans are incapable of making commitments to the community, family, causes, ideals, or marriage. It does mean, however, that such commitments are personal choices arising out of an ingrained orientation to individualism. We choose what we will be committed to and what we will not.

Our choices may arise out of either utilitarian individualism or expressive individualism. *Utilitarian individualism* is concerned with the utility or the return on one's personal choices. So, for example, a person takes a political position or votes a certain way based upon the potential benefits to that person. This is not to say that there are not people who vote on the basis of an ideology or worldview bigger than one's own needs, but in the current state of our country, business people generally vote Republican and the poor (if they vote) generally vote Democrat. They vote based upon what they perceive is in their best interests. Another example of utilitarian individualism is that a woman may join a congregation, not out of a desire to have her life reoriented, but out of a desire to get her child a good moral education. I once had a self-professed atheist who taught Sunday school—she really knew her stuff!—and had her kids enrolled in Sunday school because she thought a religious education for them was important.

Expressive individualism is not concerned so much with the payoff of one's choices but is primarily concerned with how one's choices offer opportunity for the expression of one's unique self. Thus, a person might become involved with a congregation simply for the purpose of expressing his or her musical gifts through the choir. It is not unusual for congregations to have several people singing in their musical groups who are not members but who have wonderful gifts for music and wish to express them.

The beauty of Bellah and his colleague's work is that it exposes how individualism has been a particular aspect of the American soul from the very genesis of this country. The U.S. Declaration of Independence holds up the worth of "all people," says that all have "inalienable rights," which include, "life, liberty, and the pursuit of happiness." It is telling that the framers of the Declaration of Independence understood happiness less as a state of being than as something to be pursued.

Individualism has served to permeate and inform every aspect of the American story, whether it is in the literature of the American transcendentalist writers like Walt Whitman, the wisdom of Benjamin Franklin, the fierce independence that marked much of the settlement of this country, especially the westward expansion, or a doctrine such as Manifest Destiny that presupposes an expansionist purpose for America in the world. The ethic of individualism was at the core of the 2003 unilateral decision to make a preemptive strike against Iraq. Despite international objections, the United States went ahead with the attack. This is not to say that every American supported this decision, but the decision to attack exposes the notion that we will generally follow our own perceived self-interests.

To be clear, America did not invent the ethic of self-interest. It is part of the basic human drama. The point here is that individualism in American life is deeply rooted in our historical beginnings and has been highly valued and vigorously defended as an ethic. Thus, Americans generally carry special senses of entitlement, exception, and personal power when it comes to participating in the human drama.

With a sense of cosmic specialness already deeply ingrained in the American soul, the decade of "the Sixties" became the crucible out of which a much more pronounced and obvious form of individualism would emerge and began to shape the American culture. The pioneers for this development are those of the baby boom generation. Boomers took individualism and turned it into a whole new cultural art form.

An Ethic of Self-Fulfillment

I am a baby boomer, and I must confess that even as a boomer I am weary of the attention my generation has received. More than any other American generation, boomers have been scrutinized, evaluated, written about, kowtowed to, celebrated, and scorned. People pay attention to our values, political choices, spiritual lives, tastes in restaurants and clothing, health issues, savings and retirement accounts, where we might be moving to, and when we might begin to die off. That boomers have received such attention is evidence to the huge role this generation has played and continues to play in shaping the American cultural landscape. If you also are weary of all the print and noise associated with the boomers, you had better continue to get used to it. Aside from being the largest living generation in America—some seventy million strong and representing 40 percent of the adult population—boomers' participation and influence on American life shows no signs of abating. Based upon studies of boomers and their relative vitality, health, life expectancy, and current role in American life, one can reasonably expect them to be the dominant generation for at least the first third of the twenty-first century and perhaps longer. This influence is not only felt in the sheer size of the baby boom generation; in addition, the boomer orientation to life and the world has also captured the subsequent generations, especially the Gen Xers (those born from 1966 to 1975, originally named the "baby busters" because of a drop-off in the birth rate). Rather than departing from boomer values and attitudes, Gen Xers seemingly have sharpened them. Their outward personas may be choreographed differently, but sometimes I experience Xers as being more boomer than boomers. They are often like boomers on steroids!

In order to understand how we boomers became who we are, one must pay attention to their generational experience.

The Generational Experience

My parents grew up in the Great Depression. They were each ten years old when the stock market crashed in 1929. Their teenage years were spent in a time of great economic hardship. Because of this experience, financial security was always important to them, up to the time they died. Indeed, my mother could weather just about anything, but dips and uncertainty in the financial markets gave her an extra dose of anxiety.

The idea that a generation can have a collective experience that serves to shape its beliefs, attitudes, and values is a finding of sociologists such as Karl Mannheim and others.[3] Mannheim's work was instrumental in giving shape to Wade Clark Roof's study of boomers, *A Generation of Seekers.*[4] The experience of people when they are in their teens and early twenties, especially world events, social upheavals, disasters, and the like, have a lasting influence on their lives. The experience serves to shape how they will perceive the world and participate in it. Boomers will be forever identified with their generational experience with "the Sixties." After the tumultuous events and social reengineering arising out of "the Sixties," few things would be the same in America. For sure, not all boomers shared the same experience. First-wave boomers (those born between 1946 and 1955) generally identify more deeply with "the Sixties" experience than their younger counterparts. And among the huge boomer generation, there is certainly diversity within the "collective experience." Nevertheless, the collective experience as a whole changed America.

Attitudes and Values

As boomers have journeyed though life, a collective sense of power has remained as a part of their sense of self, particularly among the first-wave boomers. After all, from their perspective, they ended a war in Vietnam. They achieved racial integration. They got a United States president to resign. And the more radical boomers, whose passions galvanized into what became known as "the movement," seemingly stood over against every social value of the previous generations. They not only helped to spawn a drug cult and an openly "do your own thing" attitude toward matters like sex, hindsight tells us that the movement also served to help engineer some needed and healthy social change, not the least of which was the gender revolution. Were it not for the movement, would many of our church bodies have ever gotten around to finally ordaining women? Admittedly, the gender revolution still has much more work to do, but were it not for the movement, would the gifts and passions of women play as prominent role in the whole of American life, from the classroom to the boardroom, as they do today? Not to be blind to the stubborn and nasty forms of intolerance in pockets of our culture today, but were it not for the movement, would our culture be as tolerant as it is? Would our culture be as rich as it is with religious pluralism and the cross-fertilization of ethnic diversities? That boomers carry a sense of collective power is understandable.

With this sense of power among boomers also came an ethic of suspicion and skepticism. Because of their youthful battle with "the establishment" and the scars many experienced, boomers gifted the culture with a distrust of institutions and authority. Along with this distrust came skepticism toward any universal claim of truth. Emerging from the boomer experience of "the Sixties" and taking fuller expression with the dawn of postmodernism is the notion that what is true is "what is true for me." Experience is valued more than the facts. Boomer-shaped postmoderns do not come into the church's arena as totally trusting souls ready to have the church fill them up with truth that will enter into their consciousness uncritically. They are not like a car pulling up to the gasoline pump. They are more like someone going to the village market in a third-world country, not with cash in their hands but with their experiences as barter. They come to the church's arena, shaped by their own experience, and expect—no, make that *demand*—that their experience be taken with ultimate seriousness and put into dialogue with the church's story. The church's story and their experience of it must have traction with the stories they bring to the table. The test of authenticity for postmoderns entering the church is whether or not the church is credible in dealing with their own real lives and issues.

The need for the experiential and participatory in boomer-shaped postmoderns reveals the depth to which they enter into the church's arena with something at stake. Although there are a variety of historical and sociological takes on the boomer experience and how that generational experience is nuanced in the culture, a general consensus exists that the overarching ethic with

which boomers have served to shape today's culture is a shift
from an ethic of self-denial to an ethic of self-fulfillment. But we
need to be careful here. Despite the lyrics of Madonna, a self-
proclaimed boomer symbol who celebrated her identity as a
"material girl" valuing wealth and material things, and despite
the labeling of boomers as the "me generation," equating self-
fulfillment as outlandish greed and self-centeredness for the
whole of the boomer-shaped world is a mistake. This is not to
say that boomers have not introduced into the culture new forms
of narcissism and self-absorption, but the "me generation" ste-
reotype has been overplayed.

The cultural move from self-denial to self-fulfillment means
that boomer-shaped postmoderns participate in life guided by
an internal gyroscope that places great importance on to what
they will give themselves and what they will not. They want "to
get something out of" their marriages, their careers, their raising
of children, and their churches. They join a fitness center, participate in psychotherapy groups, and sign up for a Saturday work
project with Habitat for Humanity because they expect something in return. Guided by utilitarian and expressive individualism, they generally do not give themselves to something simply
because they are expected to do so. What they give themselves to
must be relevant to their lives.

Authenticity deeply matters. "The Sixties" experience took
the word *hypocrite* and relegated it to one of the most despised of
personal labels. To be labeled a hypocrite was a personal affront
worse than death itself. There must be a sense of authenticity
between the confessed inner values one holds and the outer life
one lives. So, as the twentieth century entered its twilight years, a
cultural proverb took shape—"If you are going to talk the talk,
then you need to walk the walk." Because authenticity so deeply
matters, people shaped by boomer values need something to
believe in and something that matters to which they give themselves. But they are going to do it their way. The kingdom of self
is a heavily fortified kingdom.

The deep need to take control of one's life and to have things
one's own way is the fuel that drives the American pursuit of a

lifestyle. The word *lifestyle* is relatively new on the American scene. From my experience it has come to mean the convergence of such things as geographical location, home, setting, family, career, material possessions, activities, interests, leisure, commitments, future plans and hopes, and spirituality that collectively together "feel right." In order to feel right the lifestyle has to be authentic. The outward ways in which the life is lived must be consistent with one's inner values.

The challenge the church faces is that within one's lifestyle matrix the role of the church is usually just one of the many components contributing to that lifestyle. In triaging of the various components in order of importance, the church might rise to one of the higher levels in the personal or family food chain, but it is still only a component. This compartmentalized thinking means that instead of the church and its sacred story being the organizing principle that informs, gives shape, and holds together a lifestyle, the lifestyle is what is finally served. After all, *I* am in charge, and *I* will choose what is right for *me*.

Cracks in the Kingdom of Self

The track record of postmoderns exposes that at the end of the day we may not really know what is right for us. The evidence seems to say that ours is a pretty broken culture. Some of the evidence of our brokenness is right out there for all of us to see— homelessness in the inner cities, drug trafficking among our kids, marriages that are failing in epidemic proportions, bankruptcies becoming all the more commonplace, massive corporate greed in boardrooms, dishonesty in high places, high school shootings, teenage suicide, and our social-service agencies overburdened with the tasks of placing abused kids in foster homes, securing parents for unwanted newborns of teenagers, and attending to the needs of the aging living on the fringes. Other evidence is not so obvious. People who on the outside appear to have it all together endure lives of intense stress, meaninglessness, and silent desperation.

"Something Is Missing"

Perhaps the hidden pain of our brokenness was the motivation for the couple who approached me on our church lawn and confessed, "Something is missing." It is a good bet that this hidden pain is carried by many people who venture into any of the congregations in our culture today. Something is indeed missing, and our sophisticated systems of denial conspire against us to be brutally truthful with the depths of our predicament. Our systems of denial deceive us into thinking that by remaining in charge of our lives, we can orchestrate ways to heal ourselves. We may perceive that a faith community might offer something useful. Perhaps we approach the faith community with the mind-set of a deal. "I'll come to worship, and you'll make me feel good." Perhaps a cause might be helpful. "I can get so caught up in a new crusade, and it will take my mind off of my own problems. Or, maybe what I need is some solid spiritual advice. Surely there is some thirty-day spiritual program that will radically change my life."

Make no mistake about it. The stress under which many live in this age is profound. The kingdom of self is troubled. Never-mind the disconnection from a rich theological story of hope, promise, and healing that serves to anchor people. We live in an age where we are disconnected from each other. Perhaps the most serious development in the America experience is the collapse of a sense of community. Addressing this crisis, Harvard professor Robert Putnam, in his book *Bowling Alone*, lays out a thorough and sobering assessment of the collapse of community in America and demonstrates its disastrous effects on our well-being. [5] The increasing disconnection from one another has worked to jettison fundamental bonds that are essential for the happiness, health, and safety of a community. This is most certainly why the "need for community" is the most frequently expressed motivation people give for entering into our new-member processes.

Increased mobility in our economic climate has meant that people move from one community to another, often long distances from extended family and close friends. Frequently, a family move means that somebody suffers a big loss. One spouse may have to forsake a great job and start all over in the new setting. Kids have to leave friends, their sports teams, or another group of strong bonds to start all over in a new community. Making new friends with strong emotional bonds in a mobile society is not easily done. Many people cannot identify one person outside of their families or within the community in which they live whom they can name as a "best friend." Best friends are people from another time and from another place.

We live in an age where the long commute to and from the workplace is becoming all too normal, eating up precious time for being connected to others. Technology has afforded the possibilities of more and more people working out of an office in their homes. Working out of the home means that they can go days without face-to-face interaction with others. They also may be teaming with others whom they will never meet in person. When I have a technical problem with my personal computer, I do not take it down to a local repair store and speak with someone I know. I have an extended warranty. I dial a toll-free number and get a person who speaks English with a heavy Indian accent—which shouldn't be surprising, since I am actually talking to someone in India. My computer manufacturer, for economic reasons, has located their entire technical services department outside of the United States.

The age of multichannel television and home entertainment systems sporting theater-quality picture and audio for DVDs, pay-per-view movies or sports events means that we spend lots of time sequestered in our homes in front of a screen rather than in activities and conversations with others. If we are not sitting in front of an entertainment center, we then might be sitting before a computer, surfing the Internet. The Internet means that any of us can virtually buy anything we want, book any travel, or engage in any kind of conversation without having to be face-to-face with anyone. Most houses built in the last thirty years, especially in suburban subdivisions, no longer have front porches. Instead, they have back decks facing a yard that is likely protected by a solid fence, which allows their residents to cut themselves off from their neighbors and people on the street.

Because we are often disconnected from extended families and loved ones, a significant illness or death creates a particular crisis. Time, distance, and other obligations barricade us from the healing power of being in the presence of those we love and who love us. Three-day and five-day quick-fix encounters are not enough. And when we are grieving, we grieve mostly alone because the people where we work and live know little to nothing about the death that happened in our own family five states away.

Attempts to create community in this highly mobile and fragmented culture are not easy. Despite the best intentions, too many of the participants are also caught up in the "rat race."

The Rat Race

Next to mobility, perhaps the most obvious aspect for the collapse of community and meaningful engagement with others, according to Putnam, is "pervasive busyness."[6] "I don't have enough time" is often the cry of many for their failure to participate in things. The issue is not that time has been stolen. Rather, it expresses the time vise in which people find themselves when multiple issues and decisions converge: commuting distances; both spouses choosing to work (which later evolves into both spouses *having* to work because of other lifestyle choices); pressures with work, both self-imposed and imposed by an economy where workplaces demand more and more from their people; and the shuffling of children to and from day-care arrangements or school and around to the various activities they have signed onto. There is no time for participating in life-giving connections with others because too many have over-scheduled themselves. Their lives are seemingly constantly cluttered. Cell phones, voice mail, e-mail, pagers, PDAs, and handheld wireless communication devices were supposed to offer more freedom and control over one's life. Instead, they have served to add to the daily agenda, often creating unwanted distractions, and make it even more difficult to unplug from the "rat race." Get people talking and they confess to feeling constantly "hurried." They have trouble being truly committed to anything because they seem to be involved, time-wise, in just about everything.

Some live under enormous pressure. Pursuing the American Dream, many are constantly dealing with forces that reward achievement and punish failure. Their experience has told them that they could be "downsized" or relocated without cause. Wanting desperately to pay attention to their families, they are often asked to travel regularly away from home and endure the hassles that come with traveling—flight delays, cancellations, overbookings, crowded airports, and long security lines. Because they have been inculcated into a particular American script, they know that their worth is earned and not given.

A member of my congregation is a highly successful aerospace engineer who works for one of the world's leading rocket manufacturers. His division has successfully and consecutively developed, designed, and manufactured eight new rocket models, all with unblemished launch histories. This record is unprecedented in the aerospace industry; yet, he says that the overarching message that shapes his whole division is this: "You cannot fail. If you fail, this division will be closed." Conversation with others in the construction, manufacturing, computer, software, airline, oil and gas, real-estate development, ski, marketing, publishing, news, and retail industries reveal the same mantra: "Failure is not an option."

Many of those who have given themselves to the pursuit of the American Dream are actually conspirators in their own pain. Because they coexist with others who are generally pursuing the same lifestyle, they experience their stress and pain as normalcy. Often they deceive themselves into believing that the way out of their dilemma is just simply to "try harder." They may take up a new exercise regime. They may throw themselves more into their work. They may try harder at practicing some religion. They believe that if they could just "get it right" the stress would go away. Many are exhausted from trying harder.

Self-absorbed in their own predicament, many become disconnected from the realities of the rest of the world and become nonplayers in any kind of social change. They cannot be bothered with the forces of systemic oppression. They cannot give attention to the poverty in places like Haiti, homelessness in the inner cities, and much of the sexism and racism that challenge their notion of how the world works. When they do manage to carve out some experience with their family or some experience of working on a service project through a church, they are aware that these experiences are too fleeting. They are not enough to satisfy whatever it is that "is missing."

People who then pursue a lifestyle that encompasses multiple components which collectively are supposed to "feel right" are faced with a predicament. The lifestyle does not feel right at all. Living authentically, which is of prime importance, is very evasive. Folks are acutely aware that their outer lives do not match their inner deep convictions. Some are preoccupied with self-hatred. They know their lives are a lie. Many know that they live a superficial existence with superficial relationships. There is a soul-eating inner voice within. It speaks shame to them and fosters disillusionment. Many feel stuck.

Materialism, entertainment, leisure, drugs, alcohol, sex, and privatism often serve as escapes and serve to mask their pain. Many come into a worship service not sure of what they want but know that they need "something." Because almost everything they experience in terms of relationships seems to be superficial and filled with shallow conversation, they have difficulty getting in touch with and expressing the deep pain they experience. But if one can listen to the souls of many, one discovers underneath the superficiality the existence of anger, perhaps rage, cynicism, skepticism, and even defeatism toward life. Little wonder that the four most frequently prescribed drugs in the culture address high blood pressure, high cholesterol, acid reflux disorder, and depression.

Contributing significantly to the demise is a sense of entitlement—the belief that one ought to be able to enjoy the lifestyle one seeks, that is, "I ought to have it my way." Because the envisioned lifestyle is evasive, there are deep feelings of being betrayed. Children growing up in this culture soak up the emotional toxins and loneliness of their culture. Thus, a place like Littleton, Colorado—stunningly beautiful to an outside onlooker and economically affluent—consistently sports one of the highest teenage suicide rates in the country.

The movie *American Beauty*, starring Kevin Spacey and Annette Bening, won critical acclaim and numerous awards in 1999 because it brought to the screen the huge, painful paradoxes of living the American Dream.[7] With a powerfully ironic and satiric edge, the movie carried the characteristics of both a dark comedy and a tragedy. The setting was suburbia, but it could have been just about anywhere in our fragmented culture. The screenplay shows the physically attractive couple, played by Spacey and Bening, along with their troubled and rebelling adolescent daughter, contending with the superficiality and contradictions of much of their existence. Spacey's character experiences being downsized from his job in a belittling, sterile, and uncaring way. Bening's character is obsessed with being a success at selling real estate, but in her attempts to be "successful" and to "be somebody," she experiences much humiliation and periods of great despair. The movie shows their many misguided efforts to escape their pain. Candlelight dinners with nice bottles of wine in their well-furnished suburban home are filled with banal conversations that invariably turn into predictable arguments. Each family member participates in morally reprehensible behavior with which they try to fill their inner voids. Throughout the movie, Spacey's character struggles with the notion that he is expendable. His company fires him. His spouse has an affair. His daughter despises him. His inner voice says, "I am a loser," and "I am dead." The movie ends with his complicity in his own death.

Attempts to process this movie in an adult forum went something like this: "What do you think?" "Great movie!" "Do you think you'll watch it again?" "No." "Why not?" "It hits too close to home."

The hold of the "rat race" is that it works like an addiction. We know we are on a merry-go-round and do not know how to get off of it. Instead of jumping off, we keep buying more tickets. As Paul writes in Romans, "I do not understand my own actions. For I do not do what I want, but I do the very thing I hate" (Romans 7:15).

A Consumer Search

When one's spiritual life is compartmentalized, one's relation-ship with the church is inevitably consumer based. How can it not be? If I am in charge, then I am the one who chooses. I will choose what is "right for me." Never mind that the bedrock claim of the church is not that we choose God but that God in God's amazing mercy has chosen us! But in a consumer-based culture suffering from a Constantinian hangover, this foundational piece of the church's rich soil is mainly obscured. When a congrega-tion confuses style with substance, it almost invariably comes off as having some product or experience to sell. It does not make inherently obvious the astonishing story about God and God's relationship to the world. It is in God where our hope lies and not in our choices. It is God who promises to free us from what-ever bondage might hold us. This sacred story is as radically dif-ferent from the church of the deal, cause, or spiritual programming as Galileo's claim of a spherical earth was to a world stuck in the notion that the world was flat and at the cen-ter of the cosmos.

Little wonder that the consumer-based relationship persists. The church itself conspires to keep it that way. Congregations are marketing themselves like never before. Look at the Yellow Pages. Put a critical eye to congregational advertisements in the newspapers. Surf the boom of congregational Web sites. Notice how some congregations market themselves by wanting to make sure that you know that they are different or better than another kind of church. One congregation offers a top-flight youth pro-gram. Another congregation offers the most exciting worship in town. Another offers a guarantee that their sermons will not be boring. Count the number of direct-mail pieces that come to your mailbox or the marketing pieces hung on your doorknob. See how congregational marketing has entered into television and radio spots. Notice the next time you are in a congregation how that congregation's literature, welcoming strategies, and visi-tor follow-up may feel too much like a sales job. The marketing of the church in America covers all expressions of the church—

Roman Catholic, mainline, and nondenominational. Now there are even marketing efforts to recruit pastors and priests for the church.

And what effect does the reality of a plethora of different denominations and nondenominational congregations have on reinforcing a consumer-based relationship to the church? How does a person not experience all these choices as different name-brands of churches? And what is the effect when congregations market the different styles of worship services they offer—for example, "traditional at 8:00 A.M., contemporary at 9:30 A.M., and blended at 11:00 A.M.?" Doesn't the church seem to be saying, "Have it your way?"

In this kind of climate the church cannot help but be perceived as something that essentially is offering a lifestyle component. I cringe when I watch well-meaning promotional videos from my own church body in which a pastor's face appears on the screen and says, "The church is its programs." Those vital congregations serving as advance scouts for a new day in the church know that the church is not its programs. The church is simply the church—a community who is immersed in the ancient and authentic story of the life, death, and resurrection of Jesus Christ. Being immersed in the story, by nature it enjoys an ethos that heals, restores, and gives life. Many of the vital congregations I know of have begun to exorcise the word *program* from their vocabularies. The word *program* communicates an activity designed to meet some sort of utilitarian or expressive need. When the church gathers for worship, it is not a program. It is simply what the church does. When I sit down with my wife and share a meal, it is not a program. It is simply what we do together. When the church cares for the sick, gathers in small groups, takes youth away on retreats, it is not a program. It is what a community grasped by the gospel does.

There has been much spoken and written in the last two decades on church renewal and revitalization that extols the strategy of program development. The logic is that if a congregation can develop just one outstanding program—a preschool, an after-school care center, a center for teens, a food bank, or whatever—the development of that program and its payoff with the culture will lead to renewal. The central thesis of this book demands that the path to renewal lies not in the development of programs. Rather, it lies in paying attention to the very rich soil of the church, recovering it, and bringing it to life. Paying attention to programs can no more bring about sustainable vitality than giving a new paint job to and putting new seats in a worn-out 1956 Ford with 250,000 miles on it can make the car new again. You pay attention to the core—the engine, the drive train, and the structure. The last thing our overscheduled, tired, fragmented, and quick-fix-seeking culture needs is another program. *They need the church!*

Chapter Three

A Rebirthing

A few years ago my wife and I spent some time in Spain. On the afternoon of June 29th we pulled into the ancient town of Segovia where we had hotel reservations for the night. Like most ancient towns and cities in Europe, at the center of the oldest section is a plaza—the Plaza Mayor. Our little hotel was on the plaza. Also like many ancient towns in Spain, dominating the plaza is a huge medieval structure—the Cathedral of Segovia. Severely damaged in the fifteenth century during the War of Communities, it was rebuilt under Emperor Charles I of Spain and stands today as one of Spain's most emblematic Gothic churches. It is a stunningly imposing piece of architecture. One can only imagine the vision, creativity, faith, and massive labor it took to build such an awe-inspiring building.

The Gothic presentation of this cathedral and its carvings, artwork, sculptures, and ecclesial symbols bear witness to the power and influence of medieval Roman Catholicism. The place demands reverence and respect. It is also a reminder of the forces of fear the medieval church held over the people. There is little, if anything, about this cathedral that would suggest that God is a God of grace, love, and mercy or a God who ushers forth joy and thanksgiving among his people. Drawing upon the rhetoric of this book, everything about this cathedral speaks of the church as proffering a deal—a deal of the most ominous consequences at that. When I was in this cathedral and confronted with some of the walls filled with symbols of evil and eternal punishment, I somewhat felt like Dorothy must have felt when she first stood before the terrifying façade of the great Wizard of Oz. As we walked around this ancient town, I could not keep from speculating about the relationship between the people of Segovia today and this cathedral.

As the afternoon wore on, workers began to construct right on the plaza a huge outdoor stage with the cathedral as the backdrop, complete with high-tech lighting and a sophisticated sound system. When evening came—and darkness comes late in the summers in Spain—the entire plaza became transformed into the setting of a huge gala party. When my wife and I pulled into Segovia earlier in the day, we were ignorant to the fact that it was the day of the Festival of Saint Peter and Saint Paul. Moreover, it was a Friday. Our experience of Spaniards on this trip was that they needed little motivation to enjoy life in the evenings. Our intuition told us that this night was going to be something special. It was!

As evening fell, the plaza came alive. It seemed like the whole town converged into this center. There were young couples doing the romantic thing. There were families with small kids and with grandparents. Tables were set up all around the perimeter of the plaza in front of the many restaurants. We took a seat at one and began to notice the names of the different bars that opened onto the plaza. There was the Bar of the Immaculate Conception. There was the Bar of the Most Blessed Virgin. There was the Bar of the Blood of Christ. As the music blared and as people ate, drank, danced, and reveled in the spirit of this festival, biblical images of certain stories came to my mind—the wedding at Cana, the party thrown for the wayward younger son who came home, and the parable of the great banquet. As my wife and I soaked up the sights, sounds, taste, smells, and ambience of this evening in Spain, we felt that we had, by chance and by grace, been included in something sacred. We sensed that we were experiencing a form of Eucharist. This whole scene that sat in the shadows of a church that once thrived off of power, control, and fear was reborn into something different altogether. It was a complete and beautiful transformation. I thought of the verses from Psalm 30 that the pastor read years ago to my family on the night before my father's funeral:

> Sing praises to the Lord, O you his faithful ones,
> and give thanks to his holy name.
> For his anger is but for a moment;
> his favor is for a lifetime.
> Weeping may linger for the night,
> but joy comes with the morning.

Conceiving Anew

Our experience in Spain works as a metaphor for the task of rebirthing that the church faces in this confusing day of postmodernism and post-Constantinianism. Led by the Spirit, we are called to be midwives to a new conception of Christ for the world through the church, his body. The idea of a new conception is not new; it is in our inventory. It was at the heart of the conversation between Jesus and Nicodemus, a leader of the Pharisees.

In the third chapter of John, Nicodemus approaches Jesus. That Nicodemus approaches Jesus at night is important here. The writer of the fourth gospel frequently uses the rhetoric of light and dark and day and night to speak not only of the time of day but also to give clues about the spiritual condition of those in his stories. For example, in chapter twenty Mary Magdalene comes to the tomb early on Sunday "while it is still dark" (20:1). Two things are going to happen in Mary's world on this day, and they happen simultaneously. As the morning darkness gives way to early dawn, there is also a spiritual awakening or new dawning in Mary's consciousness. She is transformed from a grieving, confused, and troubled disciple concerned for the missing body of Jesus into one to whom the risen Lord speaks and calls by name. Having come to the tomb to attend to a dead Jesus, she now goes and declares, "I have seen the Lord" (20:18). It is a new day in more ways than one.

Nicodemus comes to Jesus "by night" (3:2), perhaps sensing himself that in the person of Jesus something wonderfully
new is beginning to dawn. After all, Nicodemus recognizes that
Jesus is one "who has come from God" (3:2) and thus he comes
searching. Jesus responds to Nicodemus saying that no one is
able to "see" the kingdom of God without being "born from
above" (NRSV). The Greek word, *ánothin*, has multiple mean-
ings; the NRSV translates it "from above." In other translations,
it is sometimes read as "again" or "anew." Taking the meaning of
the word as a whole with all of its nuances, Jesus is telling
Nicodemus that to see what God is up to and is doing in the
person of Jesus, one must experience a rebirthing that is of God.

Nicodemus follows Jesus' assertion of the necessity of
rebirthing from above with a question. "How? Can one enter a
second time into the mother's womb and be born after having
grown old?" The image in the question is intentionally absurd.
I, a two hundred-pound male, could never have crawled back
into the womb of my hundred-pound mother! It is in the style
of classic rabbinical debate that Nicodemus is taking Jesus on
with the absurdity of Jesus' comment. The question, however,
sets up Jesus' response, "You must be born from above" (3:7). At
this point Jesus is no longer just addressing Nicodemus alone;
he is also addressing the whole of Israel, whom Nicodemus represents. This switch is lost in the translation from biblical Greek
to English. Biblical Greek has different words for the singular
and plural use of the second-person pronoun *you*. The "you" in
verse seven is plural, meaning that Jesus is not saying specifically
to Nicodemus, "you." He is saying to the whole community of
biblical Israel, "YOU." You, Israel, with all your institutionaliza-
tion of the faith, rabbinic rules, distinctions between clergy and
lay, and sacramental system of atonement for sins, must be completely reborn! The rebirth will not be of human imagination
but from above by the movement of the Spirit of God (cf. 3:8).
Remember that at the end of the Gospel of John three things
flow from the body of Jesus: blood and water after he dies (19:34)
and the Holy Spirit when he confronts his disciples on Easter
evening (20:22). From these gifts comes the birth of a new com-

munity, the church. John's Jesus is doing cultural architecture for a new community.

The womb for conceiving the church anew today cannot be from a different parent. The womb for this conception is the rich soil of the church, the very DNA in our inventory of a God who so "loved the world" (John 3:16). The womb is the ancient and authentic story of Jesus Christ, crucified and now risen. Within that womb is the metaphor that belongs to the baptized, "dying and rising." To restate again the central thesis of this book, the rebirthing of an authentic church with transformational traction with the culture is not about programs or strategies. It is about bringing to life out of the rich soil of the church the ancient and authentic story of Jesus and the construction of a faith community whose life together, passions, and character—that is, its community ethos—are constructed from the authenticity and integrity of the story. In order to rebirth the church and conceive anew Christ for the world in this opportune time to be the church, some things will have to die.

The rebirthing of an authentic church will necessarily mean putting to death the false notions of the church from the Constantinian era that still hang over the church today. The church must end the business of brokering deals, enlisting people in causes, and dispensing spiritual goods and services. The importance of paying attention to the church's ancient and authentic story became greatly amplified when the community in which I am a pastor gathered in the midst of an awful tragedy.

A Community Crisis and the Church Born Anew

As alluded to earlier in this book, our congregation was one of the "ground-zero" congregations after the Columbine High School shootings. On an evening in April 1999, our congregation held a worship service—the kind of service that pastors and congregations hope they never have to host. Under a steady drizzle on a dark night, reflecting the mood of the community, people streamed into our worship center that sits a mile or so west of Columbine High School in Littleton, Colorado. Kids brought their friends, clutching each other and wailing in deep grief. Some brought their Columbine soccer T-shirts and hung them over our communion rail. One group brought a Columbine yearbook and placed it on our altar. When the service began with a hymn that implored God to "pour your power" on the church, to "cure our children's warring madness," and to grant us "wisdom" and "courage" to "face" the "hour,"[1] our worship center's capacity was already filled to overflowing.

On this night we did not have answers that could provide any meaning or explanation for the carnage and evil that had engulfed the high school the day before. We offered no quick fix for the pain and the huge, aching holes in all our hearts. All we had to offer was a story—the story of Jesus Christ, the one who himself was victimized and suffered an awful death, and yet is now raised from the dead.

On this night the congregation did not experience a deal, a cause, or a form of spiritual self-help. The absence of such rhetoric was intentional and essential to the cultural architecture of our congregation. Deal language might have dealt with the question, "Why?" or sent the message, "Be sure that you are saved in case this should ever happen to you." In the days following this community disaster, there were fundamentalist groups that paraded in front of school gatherings with this "be-sure-you-are-saved" agenda. Using the tragedy to fuel a cause might have resulted in the church's making a passionate plea to take whatever steps are necessary to ensure school safety in the future and for getting guns out of the hands of kids. That important cause took on a huge life of its own in the days after without our prompting. In the language of spiritual self-help, the church might have decided to explore the different stages of grief for the purposes of instructing people on how to navigate through their grief. In that regard, tons of resources soon flowed into the community so that all students could have access to grief counselors and as many people as possible could have access to printed grief materials. Rather, intentionally being true to its self-understanding, the gathered church on this night left the deals, causes, and spiritual helps to others and instead looked death in the face, named the reality for what it was, and offered God.

Through tears that flowed in this amazing gathering, the congregation belted out another hymn at such a volume that the organist wisely chose to let the final stanza be sung *a cappella*:

> God's word forever shall abide.
> No thanks to those who fear it;
> For God himself fights by our side
> With weapons of the Spirit.
> Were they to take our house,
> Goods, honor, child or spouse,
> Though life be wrenched away,
> They cannot win the day.
> The kingdom's ours forever![2]

Following the hymn, the congregation prayed and then shared the meal of the church. In the meal, the gathered community experienced the risen Christ. He came to them in the meal as the Wounded One, as the one to whom violence had been done, and as the victim. But he came also as the Victorious One and as the one who still holds the future and the final word. The gathered community tasted his future.

When the congregation sang the final hymn, *Precious Lord, Take My Hand,* and worship ended, most of the gathering went into groups where conversation and mutual support took place until almost midnight. People knew that what they had experienced on this night was not the receipt of some helpful information. It was something altogether different.

Nothing had really changed on this night. The dead were still dead. The community still grieved. It would be a long road toward healing and renewed hope. It would be a long time before unbridled laughter would again be heard, Yet, though nothing had changed, people awakened to the reality that everything had changed. Those who came experienced transformation, what happens when God is unleashed authentically and with unashamed theological precision. Those who came brought nothing to the gathering. They were so broken they had nothing to bring, but, in the words of the fourth gospel, their experience of the faith community and the story out of which the community lives meant that they were being reborn again from above.

Putting the Church out of Business

As long as the church is in the business of deals, causes, and spiritual services, the rich soil of the church will be obfuscated. When this happens, the authentic story that infuses the church with its authority and transformational power is not just compromised. It is often totally lost. The substitution of deals, causes, and spiritual services works to create consumer relationships. Consumer relationships emerge between the church and the culture it serves, that is, its clientele. Consumer relationships also emerge between congregational members and the congregation as a whole, disclosed in either the cry of "You are not meeting our needs," or "Look at these new programs we have engineered just for you."

No doubt, people almost certainly come to the church as consumers, even for apparently good reasons—in search for the gospel on the night of a tragedy. The task of the church is that they not be left to remain as consumers. The task is to gift them with the church's rich soil that envelops them and draws them into the church's identity and calling. To do this means to put the church out of business.

Killing the Deal

Getting out of the business of cutting deals is a risky venture. Deep in the American experience and part of our ecclesial landscape is the plethora of faith communities that insist that the purpose of the church not only is to save people; it is also to help people to discern between the saved and the unsaved and to admonish people to do the kinds of things that saved people do. After all, one pastor in the Littleton community stood in his pulpit on the Sunday after the high school shootings and proclaimed, "If Eric Harris and Dylan Klebold had been saved, they would not have done what they did."

In the deal's worldview, the world is a sinful and evil place. It is like a huge ocean liner that is sinking into the abyss of eternal damnation and darkness. The purpose of the church is to rescue as many people as possible from this disaster and get them prepared for life in the next world, heaven. Almost invariably the formula for getting saved includes making a personal decision for Christ. Christ becomes one's personal Lord and Savior.

This way of relating to God is very Constantinian. By the decision that I make, I end up co-opting God to be on my side. The biggest benefit is that by my decision I have gotten God on my side for eternity. Also, the more I become convinced of the benefits of my personal decision for Christ and the character of my saved status the more I may assume some personal spiritual power when it comes to the agenda of God. Thus, I can pass judgment on others whose lifestyles are different from mine, conclude that people who identify with other faiths are "going to hell," and in the extreme, become radically dogmatic on what is the will of God and what is not. Often that dogmatic approach becomes public through religious leaders interpreting current events to the greater public from their own perception of God's activity in the world or through their trying to push their convictions about the will of God onto society. Why else would some of our most conservative Christian fundamentalist leaders argue that the September 11, 2001 terrorist attacks on our country were possible because God had removed his protective shield from us due to the decay of our culture? Why else would a bishop publicly condemn pro-life politicians and issue a statement that calls on communion to be withheld from them and from anyone who votes for them?

We need to kill the deal because the deal itself actually kills. It certainly served to injure a young man named Bill who approached me while he was home for the Christmas holidays. He had joined a parachurch movement while in college and had become a leader in it. For three years, he attended weekly Bible studies, rallies that "saved people for Christ," and national conventions. During his senior year, he had become friends with a student from Iran. They were not close friends by any means but did do some studying together because they were in the same classes. The campus leader of this movement, the "missionary" as he was called, approached Bill one day and asked Bill to "be careful." He had noticed that Bill had an Iranian friend. He said to Bill, "You know that your Muslim buddy is going to hell." When Bill heard these words, it sent him into a personal crisis. He literally obsessed over what the missionary had told him. Bill was a very bright young man, carrying a hefty GPA while securing a double major in computer science and mathematics. His critical thinking skills absorbed the words of the missionary and led him to reject completely what he assumed Christianity to be.

When we met for lunch, Bill said to me, "Pastor, I no longer believe in God." My response, as I usually respond in such instances was, "Well, Bill, tell me about the god you do not believe in, and I probably don't believe in that god either." The conversation gave wonderful opportunity to expose the terrible misgivings and unfaithfulness of the gospel as a deal.

One of the oldest human misconceptions is that we can somehow save ourselves by our choices, beliefs, and actions. Supposedly, as this line of thinking goes, the practice of religion will make us better people (which it indeed might and can do). Equally important, the practice of religion will supposedly give us some sort of advantage in the game of life. Christianity in this guise of a deal is inherently mechanistic and means that the practicing of the Christian religion will somehow jimmy the cosmic system—a system filled with good and bad luck—in one's favor. If practicing a religion has significant payoffs and if jimmying the system in such a way is possible, then, of course, the right practicing of religion must weigh heavily. The radical claim of Christianity is that the church, in its essence and faithfulness to its story, actually dares to look the deal in the eye and announce the end of religion.[3]

The story that grounds the church is not that we are particularly good, have undertaken some nice projects, or achieved some protection against bad happening to us. The church bears witness not to the choices we make but to the choice that God has made and continues to make. The story that grounds the church is that God is good and is a God who comes back and keeps coming back to a world that rejects him. The biblical witness is that the world crucifies Jesus and his disciples desert him, and yet the risen Jesus comes back to meet them on the road to Emmaus, opening again the scriptures to them and breaking bread in their midst (Luke 24:13-35). He orders the first apostles to announce to the ends of the earth the "forgiveness of sins" (Luke 24:47).

The only decision that matters is God's. The Bible even teaches us not to trust the decisions that we make because we cannot escape the reality that we are always sinners. We are laden with our own self-serving agendas and are sometimes even astonished at our own actions or failure to act (cf. Romans 7). When I kept telling Bill over lunch that the notion that God's salvation and a future with God have nothing to do with any human religious decision and that it was all about God, he was struggling mightily. The words he was hearing from me contradicted everything he had learned and absorbed in the church-as-deal paradigm that had shaped him. So I told him a story.

For high school, I attended The McCallie School in Chattanooga, Tennessee, an all-male college preparatory school with a Christian emphasis where I was a boarding student. Every year we had a period called "religious emphasis week." Religious emphasis week was a time when classes and other activities would be shortened so that we could gather each day in order for some outside speaker to fill us with religion. In anticipation of this week, we students all complained in our dorm rooms. We said that we would not listen. We were not going to have some hotshot outsider come in and ram religion down our throats. We made a pact together: we would not listen.

Despite our stubborn resolve to resist, the preacher was a powerfully engaging speaker. On the first day, he got our attention. On Tuesday, he began to paint the picture of what happens to those who do not accept Jesus. By Wednesday night, everybody in the dorm was a little scared. We were all talking about what the preacher was saying. On Thursday, his last day in our chapel, the preacher concluded by offering an altar call. About half of the student body stampeded to the front of the chapel.

I was part of the stampede. That day I got down on my knees, confessed what a wretched human being I was, accepted Jesus as my Lord and Savior, and invited Jesus to live in my heart. When I finished telling that story to Bill, I said, "And you know what? A week later I was still just a fourteen-year-old kid, thinking the kind of thoughts fourteen-year-olds have, going through the religious motions in our chapel, and I could not tell if what happened on my knees in the presence of the good reverend had made any difference in me at all. My salvation cannot depend upon my decision because I can't trust my decision."

The deal kills because the North American landscape is filled with people who will not go near a church because they have been deeply injured by the church as deal passing judgment on them. The deal burdens us with religion, and religion kills. The deal kills because in order to buy into the deal one has to look with pity or suspicion on those who are outside of one's religion. The deal kills because that pity and suspicion often turns to disrespect, hatred, and violence. The deal kills because it fosters self-righteousness, and self-righteousness eventually leads to the judgment of others. Judgment deeply injures. The deal kills because in one's neuroses one not only worries about whether one has done everything one is supposed to do; one also worries about the salvation of those one loves. One cannot be sure, you see, if they have done all the right things to be saved.

The church that bears witness to the Jesus who came not to "condemn" the world but to "save" it (John 3:17), and that holds to the scriptures which proclaim that we are so saved solely by grace that boasting is prohibited (Ephesians 2:8-9) must bury forever all notions of the gospel as being some sort of deal. It must birth again Jesus to the world not as the main player in the deal but as our unshakable hope. I repeat: the only decision that matters is God's, and God has already acted in Jesus Christ.

As we have now entered into the third millennium and face global ecological challenges of immense proportions with the potential for some ominous outcomes, the deal will get us nowhere. If the purpose of this life is to do all the right things to ensure getting into the next life, then why should we really care about this world? Why should we be good stewards of the environment? This world is just temporary, is it not? The real world is yet to come. And as a nation "under God," are we not entitled to the vast proportion of resources we consume? Is that not part of the special blessing God has showered on us Americans?

The deal is contributing to the killing of our planet. For the integrity of the church and for the power of the church's witness, the church has to kill all deals.

End the Causes

In the world of the Holy Roman Empire, causes were necessary to advance the agenda of the Empire. Causes had support for their action in the clear will of God, at least according to the emperor. The church was supposed to take up a certain cause because God desired it. In the rebirthing of the church today that puts an end to causes, it is important to distinguish between the church's witness to the world and activism. The church as cause today is really, for the most part, a form of activism.

The church as a cause today does not so much focus on Jesus as Lord and Savior as much as on Jesus as an activist. This church has so borne the assault of modernity on its very identity that it no longer takes with ultimate seriousness the church's essential claims. Perhaps the weight of the historical-critical method of exegesis has crushed some people's faith in the authority of the scriptures. Perhaps awareness of the slippery enterprise to uncover more fully the historical Jesus has prompted doubt. Indeed, some have said that the Jesus Seminar[4] is modernity's last and most vicious assault on the Jesus of the Christian gospel. Perhaps sermons and church-body agendas that have overly focused on social change rather than on the proclamation of the gospel have taken their toll.

Whatever the cause, modernity's assault on the church's claims has resulted in countless people who identify themselves with the church yet who have reconciled themselves to a plausibility that maybe Jesus is not who the church claims he is and that he did not rise from the dead. Perhaps instead wild dogs actually took his body. Nevertheless, these people claim church

membership and pay attention to Jesus because they are fasci-
nated by his teachings and believe that Jesus did many good
things. In this view of Jesus, it is very difficult to distinguish the
person of Jesus as being fundamentally different from people
like Gandhi, Martin Luther King Jr., or Mother Teresa. All of these
people sought to change the world, alleviate human suffering
and injustice, and are persons to emulate.

The church as cause has great appeal for many, even though
it operates as functional atheism. Community or global action
is taken up in the name of the cause. People do not need to get
bogged down in a bunch of religious rhetoric or rituals nor be
burdened with the intellectual embarrassment of them. They are
simply free to give themselves to meaningful projects.

The church as cause or the activist church is a bad idea because, just like the church as a deal, this kind of church encour-
ages us to put too much faith in ourselves.[5] Our projects will not
save us. Our schemes will not save us. More people were killed
in the wars of the twentieth century than in the wars of all periods before. The twenty-first-century death count may be even
higher. The global gap between the rich and the poor continues
to widen. The world community finds it impossible to unite with
a shared strategy to face the grave concerns over global warning
and the environment. Despite all the deep investments we make
in the human immortality project, the death rate is still one death
per person. This is not to say that supporting cancer research, or
recycling cans and glass bottles, or paying attention to physical
fitness are not important. They are. The problem with the church's
identity and calling being turned into a cause is that it puts the
emphasis on humans and our good works. The church witnesses
not to us but to a God who brings light from darkness, raises the
dead to new life, and is at work, through Jesus Christ, reconciling the world to himself.

The congregation I serve is not deeply committed to Haiti
because we have people who need to be involved in some des-
perate cause. For sure, the folks who have given themselves to
the Haiti initiative are filled with compassion, but they do it out
of a sense of witness. They understand that we are called to be in

Haiti because of the gospel. Inscribed on the altar in our worship center are the words that begin the vision of the prophet's
eschatological banquet, Isaiah 25:6:

> On this mountain the Lord of hosts will make for all peoples
> a feast of rich food, a feast of well-aged wines . . .

With this vision of cholesterol-rich food and the finest wines
comes some amazing promises: God will destroy garments of
mourning because they will no longer be needed. God will "swal-
low up death forever." God will wipe away tears from "all faces."
God will take away the disgrace of his people from all the earth.
The prophet writes that the "Lord has spoken"; therefore, it is as
good as done (Isaiah 25:7-9)!

When the prophet writes "all people" and "all faces," there
is no distinction between a saved group and an unsaved group.
"All" means *all*. There is no identification with those who took
up the cause and those who did not. God will simply act. And if
alleviating human suffering and removing the disgrace of poverty are promised and guaranteed, we who are the church must
participate in the future as if it is already happening. We go to
Haiti as a witness to the future promised by God. To disconnect
this needful initiative or any other initiative of positive social
change from the grounding of the gospel is to obscure the gospel itself. This is a challenge for the church who deeply loves the
world and yet lives under a Constantinian hangover in a skepti-
cal postmodern world.

Recognizing and naming the life-killing nature of the church
as deal and the passion of those who take up causes is not to
suggest that the church's task is to exorcise such people from our
membership. People who carry the church as deal or cause in
their consciousness are going to be in our midst and participate
in the church's mission. The atheist who once taught in our Sunday School had a cause. She thought that teaching children about
the Christian faith, though she did not believe it, was good. She
was good for our congregation! She was good for the kids. She
was also good for me. You become very careful in how you choose
your words when in the presence of a bright, articulate, and criti-

cally thinking atheist! It is also a mistake to assume that all "deal" people are religious conservatives and "cause" people are liberals. Sometimes the cause flows from the deal, that is, saving as many people as possible. Or the cause can become the deal, that is, conducting acts of mercy are necessary for eternal salvation. Also, the very presence of diverse people in the church is a witness to the gathering activity of God. God gathers not just those who have passed a theological litmus test; God gathers because God is at work reconciling the world to Christ and thus bringing life to it. The church's task is then not to exclude or eliminate people. The church's task is to be faithful to its authentic witness.

No More Chaplaincy to the Culture

The cultural assumption that the church exists to meet people's needs is a very Constantinian precept. It assumes that the church and the culture are both on the same page. The church does not have a radical story that defines reality over and against cultural worldviews. Instead, it presents the church as more like a religious store: Membership is okay if that's your thing, but the church exists to meet my needs, doesn't it? If I happen to come and worship at the church, it ought to be uplifting. Moreover, I should have choices about the style I want—traditional, contemporary, or blended. The sermon should be something that I can apply to my daily life. If I need to have my child baptized, the church should do it. If I have a wedding to plan, I should be able to use the church. If my teenager is giving me problems, I should be able to send the kid to the church's youth group. I expect the church to have a number of programs to meet my needs.

In January 2000 I did some research on some forty-eight adults who were entering into our new-member preparation process. I wanted to try to discern their understanding of the nature of the church as well as get some sort of insights about their perceptions of God. The research confirmed two things: first, they had many wants they identified—community, youth groups, personal spiritual needs, inspirational worship, to name a few. Their answers were completely consistent with forms of expressive or utilitarian individualism. Second, few connected the church to the death and resurrection of Jesus. Except for the few who did make the connection, the majority articulated God in the typology of the gospel as deal. The next most prevalent responses equated the church as the cause typology. The rest of the responses identified the church and God with some form of sentimentality, such as "God is love." Stanley Hauerwas and William Willimon warn that sentimentality is really "how unbelief is lived out; that when the gospel is reduced to sentiment, we are left with no gospel."[6] God is not much into sentiment.

The problem with the church as a cultural chaplain is that it trivializes God. It trivializes the passion and tenacity of God to get back what belongs to God. It trivializes the suffering of God in Jesus Christ. It trivializes the triumph of God in the resurrection of Jesus over everything that would cheapen, fragment, or destroy our lives. It too often subjugates itself to proffering a feel-good spirituality, and a feel-good spirituality will always trivialize sin and the depth of the human predicament. It seemingly gives itself to narcissistic needs because much of what the church does seems to be more about self-help than the radical call to discipleship.

The church I serve is so passionate about being an authentic witness to the death and resurrection of Jesus Christ and, at the same time, so convinced that the culture needs to be detoxified from the effects of the Constantinian hangover that our new-member preparation process underwent a rebirth not long ago. Instead of being primarily a technical orientation to our congregation and "what Lutherans believe," it has become an adaptive journey. Through six sessions, participants experience a systematic deconstruction of the institutional Constantinian church along with its fallout and are filled up with an identity and calling of the church born again and anew out of the womb of the ancient and authentic story of the church. This process is far from perfect, but all of us involved with it know that we are onto something that holds transformational promise. Forty-five minutes into the first session in this process, the leader says to the participants, "The church does not exist to meet your needs. It exists to meet God's needs." No one has ever walked out. Our aim with this process is to prepare participants for a journey of membership that will, by the Spirit of God, transform them from consumers to passionate owners of the church's identity and calling—its mission—to be a witness to each other and the world.

Although the church does not exist to meet humanity's narcissistic needs, because the church is about meeting God's needs, immersion into the church is healing. God's agenda is aimed at the deepest of human needs and when unleashed through the church's story, it brings hope from despair, light from darkness, and life from death.

Rebirthing Community Spirituality

The bookstore's juxtaposition of the huge self-help section next to the large spirituality section speaks volumes about the spiritual hunger of our culture and the pervasiveness of American individualism in how people relate to things spiritual. It is a consumer relationship. It is driven by the desire "to get something out of it." Spirituality presumably must have some usefulness for the individual. One's relationship with God is deemed to be personal; it is about "God and me" or "Jesus and me." This personal paradigm is to be expected in a culture in which Jesus has been defined as a "personal Lord and Savior." This personal aspect is almost the sole emphasis among a matrix of contemporary Christian songs dominated by lyrics that proclaim "My Jesus . . . my Savior . . . my debt" and the like.

Among many people, one's relationship with God is also deeply private. Private spirituality not only has difficulty in seeing a useful connection with a congregation; private spirituality can also see a connection with the church as harmful. So we have a culture with legions of people who privately will confess belief in God but also will say, "I gave up on the church a long time ago," or, "What I do with my life is strictly between God and me and is nobody else's business." Congregations often hear that last comment when the annual pledge drive comes around.

The Church Gathers Because of God

If people do indeed seek out a congregation for a church home, the number-one reason, at least from the data gathered in our new-member process, is a need for community. In our world of fragmented, disconnected, and stressed-out lives, people long for social interaction with others. Human beings are not meant to be alone. The need to belong is great. So strong is the need to belong that people seek out a church home as a consumer need. The experience of "community" is a consumer desire driven by both utilitarian and expressive individualism. Yet, the experience of community for the sake of the experience itself is not the fundamental reason why the church gathers. The church gathers not because of us or our consumer needs. The church gathers because of God. God gathers the church.

God gathers the church for God's purposes. The community that gathers is about God and what God is up to in the world. The community gathers as the church and does what the church does as a witness to God's agenda and activity in the world. The next chapter of this book will speak more fully on what it means for a church community to be a "witness," but the trajectory of the discussion that follows here is toward lifting up the primacy of the community's relationship with God.

The Hebrew scriptures testify to the unique identity and calling of the community of Israel. Out of the backdrop of human brokenness and rebellion against God, God calls Abraham to be the forebear of a new community—later to be named Israel—who will ultimately be a "light to the nations" (Isaiah 42:6) and through whom "all the families of the earth shall be blessed" (Genesis 12:3). The constellation of narratives, wisdom literature, and prophetic genre in the Hebrew scriptures together tell the story of Israel's struggles with being true to its identity and calling. They also speak of God's unrelenting faithfulness in the face of Israel's challenges. God never gives up on God's community.

The New Testament exists because of the creation of a new community birthed out of Israel and who gathers in the name of Jesus. They gather and do what they do because of being grasped by the Spirit of the living God who raised Jesus from the dead. The risen Jesus will use the community for God's purposes. "You will be my witnesses" (Acts 1:8). The very understanding of the Greek word *ekklesia*, which is translated "church" in the English versions, is a people called together by God out of the world to be a community gathered for a purpose. The church gathers because of God.

The Bible and a Personal Relationship with Jesus. To underscore the notion that it is the community with which God is chiefly concerned means that attention must be given to the phenomenon of the personal relationship with Jesus. Having a personal relationship with Jesus in the presumed manner that pervades our culture today is not a prevalent theme in the New Testament. This is not to say that there are not some aspects that touch on the personal. After all, Jesus calls people by name, such as Lazarus (John 11:43), and he calls individuals to be his disciples (Mark 1:16-20 and parallels). In our traditional hymnody, we sing songs that speak of our personal commitment and relationship to Christ; for example, *Just as I Am, Be Thou My Vision, I'm So Glad Jesus Lifted Me*. The psalmist also writes, "I lift up my eyes to the hills—from where will my help come? My help comes from the Lord . . ." (Psalm 121:1), or "My soul thirsts for God" (Psalm 42:2). The Psalter is the best collection of expressions of personal piety in all the scriptures, but in reading the Psalms, the reader must be aware that these collections were written as a witness for the whole community of Israel and often used as congregational hymnody and for community worship. In the New Testament expressions of personal piety are infrequent.

Whatever references there are to personal issues of faith in the New Testament, they are always within the context of the work of Jesus' gathering of the church. Almost all of what Jesus has to say in the New Testament comes at the church in the plural form of the word *you*. Jesus never speaks about taking up a personal relationship with him. He never even remotely suggests that we are to invite him into our hearts. Rather, he invites us to him by saying, "Follow me" (Mark 1:17 and parallels) and "Come to me" (Matthew 11:28). He says that his death and exaltation will draw "all people to himself" (John 12:32). Jesus says to those who become the church, "You [plural] are the light of the world" (Matthew 5:14).

Jesus and Community. Instead of advocating a personal or private relationship with Jesus, the New Testament is bathed in a fundamental assumption: the entity that bears witness to the new situation wrought by the death and resurrection of Jesus and the outpouring of the Holy Spirit is a community; indeed, a unique community. It has its own unique story, a story in tension with the story of the culture in which the church lives. New Testament scholar Gerhard Lohfink, in his book *Jesus and Community*, makes two convincing arguments that are useful here.[7] The first is that the church is not a new religion founded by Jesus. Rather, it is the gathering of a community out of the matrix of Israel, which understands itself to be the renewed Israel and is grasped by the redemptive work of Jesus through the work of the Holy Spirit. Second, the self-understanding of this community is that it is to be a "contrast society."[8] The church lives in contrast to the world around it. It has its own self-defining story, identity, worldview, sense of hope, ethics, ethos, character, and purpose that exist in tension with the world.

The relationship that matters the most to Jesus is Jesus' relationship to the church. It is to the church that Jesus makes most of his promises. At the end of Matthew, Jesus says, "I will be with you always" (Matthew 28:20). The "you" is plural. Note also how Jesus speaks about conflict management in the church (Matthew 18:15-20). Not only does he equate the work of conflict management and reconciliation in the church as also the work of heaven and something in which heaven has a big stake (verses 18-19), he says that it takes "two or three gathered in my name" for him to be present (verse 20).

In the Gospel of John, five chapters are devoted for the words of Jesus that biblical scholars have named his "Farewell Discourse" (chapters 13–17). The whole point of the discourse is to prepare the disciples for what is getting ready to happen to Jesus, and subsequently also to them. The plot to arrest Jesus is already at full bore. The setting is the final gathering of his disciples before his crucifixion. Several things important for the formation of the community happen in this discourse. Jesus recognizes the brokenness of the world and the tension with which the new community will live in relationship to the world. "If the world hates *you* [plural], remember that it hated me before it hated *you* [plural]" (15:18). He speaks of himself as being a vine and the church as the branches. There are life-and-death stakes associated with staying together as a community connected to Jesus (15:1-12). He repeatedly tells them to "love one another as I have loved you" (15:12; 13:34-35). The physical metaphor that he gives to them for this love is the footwashing (13:1-17). He makes promises: "I will not leave *you* [plural] orphaned" (14:18); "Because I live, *you* [plural] also will live" (14:19); "My peace I give to *you* [plural]" (14:27). And at the end of the discourse he prays that his disciples and the church of every age might be "one" (17:11) and have his Father's protection on them from the world (17:14ff.).

The emphasis on community is not to belittle the individual or to mean that the individual is not important. The lifting up of the value and primacy of the community actually serves to elevate the value of the individual. Paul's metaphor of the church as the "body of Christ" perhaps best illustrates this. In this special unique community, no one is indispensable (1 Corinthians 12:14-26). Each member of the body has valuable gifts (12:4-11). Each member is called to a different role within the body (12:27ff; also Romans 12:4-8; Ephesians 4:11). All are called for the purpose of "building up the body" for the work of "ministry" (Ephesians 4:12) and for the "common good" (1 Corinthians 12:7). Paul is among the first to get the idea of synergy, that the whole of the community is infinitely greater than the sum of the individuals. Spending time in the New Testament and taking it as a whole make the phenomena of the emphasis on individualism and consumer relationships with the church today more than mildly baffling.

Community and Character

In order for the church of this postmodern era to be truly authentic to the story that grounds it and the Holy Spirit who empowers it and guides it, it must rebirth itself in a consumer culture and emerge clearly as a uniquely called community. It cannot continue its institutional identity. It cannot be a collection of individuals. It must reclaim its identity as a movement of people called together by God. People cannot *belong* to the church. The people who have been baptized into the church simply *are* the church. Called by God, the church has a distinct and authentically faithful character.

Paul's description of the human body and the essentialness of each member as a metaphor for the body of Christ is especially helpful here (cf. 1 Corinthians 12:12-27). Your right hand, assuming you have one, is part of your body. It has the same DNA as the rest of your body. It does not have a choice about being a part of your body. It simply is, as are the rest of the individual parts of your body. Cut your hand off and it dies (unless there is successful reconnection surgery). Your hand is so much a part of your body, you probably are not even aware when you rest your face in it. If you play the guitar or piano, and are somewhat accomplished at it, you are probably not explicitly aware of what your right hand is doing, unless you happen to focus on it. All the parts of your body work together like a symphony. When your hand is cut, the rest of the body is affected. The nerves in your hand at the point of injury send signals to the brain that cause you to be aware of pain. Your immune system sends antibodies to the wounded area to fight infection. If the wound is not too severe, the blood system will send anticoagulants to stop the bleeding. And in order to protect the wound as it begins healing, the tissue around the cut will form a scab over it.

My right hand is essential to my body. I write, type, brush my teeth, shave, shoot a basketball, and cast a fly rod with it. To do all these things the hand does not do it alone. It must coordinate with the eye, the left hand, and the rest of the body's systems. I cannot imagine living without my right hand. I have a friend who lost his right hand in a freak accident as a boy. He does quite well without the hand. He is low-handicap golfer, plays the trumpet, is an expert downhill skier, and designs rockets for a living. He has adapted, but he would rather have his hand than not. Imagine what might be possible with both hands.

The metaphor of the body of Christ is not only helpful in understanding the essential nature of each part; it is also helpful in illuminating the nature of the church. Your body has a certain character. When you are very happy, your whole body joins in it. When you are challenged, your whole body deals with it. This is not to say that your body is never conflicted. It is. Sometimes your mind might say that you want to swim three miles, but your arms don't have the energy. Sometimes you might decide that you need to cut down on your calories, but your body starts getting shaky because you are not getting enough protein. But as a whole, as you journey through life, your body develops a certain character. When I use the word *body* here, I am being very biblical with the word. It does not mean just your physical body with all of its organs. It also means your imagination, predictable moods, tolerance to risk, sense of compassion for others, resiliency, attitude, and certain gifts of the Spirit that Paul says you have. Some of your character is given by God, such as your ability to do well at math, play music, or your extraverted, intuitive, and value-centered personality. Some of your character is developed by your experience and your response to that experience. As Romans 5:1-5 says, our character is forged by our experience. Your character is a product of stories that have been told to you, what you believe and learned to be true, and the mentoring of parents and others who invested in you. You cannot escape your character. If you do something "out of character," as the saying goes, it is a just a blip on the radar screen of your life.

The formation of your character is never about strategies, programs, or tactics. So it is with the church as the body of Christ. The Spirit of God that ushers forth from the crucified and risen Christ both gives birth to the church and forms the character of the church as an organic body of many members. The body is given a story. The truth of that story is both tested and forged in the life of the body. As the community's character is forged and the body stays immersed in the ancient and authentic story of the church, the body begins to look, feel, act, heal, and serve as Christ himself. The transformational power of the risen Christ is both present *in* the body and present *through* the body. Because of the body taking on the identity of Christ, the body exudes a character of unshakable faithfulness, strength, endurance, compassion, joy, and hopeful imagination. The body and the story become one.

Instead of giving the world deals, causes, spiritual services, programs, tactics, propositions, and arguments, what if the church instead gave the world Christ? Not to sound pious here, but the church gives the world Christ because the church gives itself, and the world experiences Christ because the world experiences the church as his authentic body proclaiming the story and living out of that story. What if congregations gave the people who sit in their pews and whose names are on their membership rolls Christ? What if instead of Christ being some ancient figure who is the purveyor of deals, the author of causes, or some sentimental spiritual guru, Christ became alive for people through the congregation's body with its breathing and its pulse? Instead of people's inviting Jesus into their hearts, Jesus would be drawing people into *his* heart. They become one with *his* body. That's where the rebirthing begins. We go back to the womb of the rich soil of the church's story and get it right this time. Constantine cannot kidnap Christ again. This time we bring out of the womb and birth an authentic body of Christ for this world in this day. The next chapter will take us to the delivery room.

Chapter Four

It's Just Church

A few years ago my congregation was preparing to conduct a very important capital-fund campaign. A mission team was formed to select the firm who would serve as a consultant to assist the congregation in its efforts. Selecting the right firm to work with a congregation in such campaigns is critical. Congregations not only need a firm that is up-to-date in the necessary expertise to speak of biblical stewardship in the postmodern world and obtain positive results; they also need a firm whose way of being is a theological and cultural fit for their particular practice and setting. The firm with the best track record in raising money may not be the best firm to select for a given effort.

On a Sunday afternoon the mission team gathered to begin conducting interviews with the two finalists in the selection process. The first firm to have their time before the selection team sent two of their top people, the president and the person whom she had personally handpicked to be our on-site consultant and, by her words, "the best in the business." Both were dressed impeccably in attire that seemed more suitable for a high-powered Wall Street gathering than for the relaxed group of individuals that gathered as a team on this Sunday afternoon. The two representatives handed out several slick marketing materials that told the story of their firm, its growth in its industry, and how they had outperformed their competitors in all kinds of settings.

After a few introductory remarks, the two asked us to pay attention to a very impressive audio-visual presentation. It gave the entire playbook on how they would conduct the campaign in our congregation and included moving testimonies from their satisfied customers. About five minutes into this presentation a member of the selection team interrupted the theatrics by saying, "Excuse me. Would you please turn that off?" The two representatives seemed confused. The president asked, "What did you say?" The team member who had interrupted repeated, "Please turn that off."

Two members of this selection team were top-level leaders in Fortune 500 companies. One member had his own firm that handled the marketing for professional sports teams in the NHL and NBA. Another was the founder of one of the country's top providers of Internet-based mortgage financing. Another was the manager of a structural-steel contractor. One was a mental-health professional. The one who had interrupted said to the puzzled people, "We don't want to be disrespectful, but we watch this kind of stuff all the time. We know how marketing works. The system of fundraising that you are laying out is no different, in its essence, from the others." I looked around the room and the rest of the team was nodding. The two representatives had a panicked look on their faces.

The spokesperson for the mission team continued, "We are gathered here this afternoon away from our own boardrooms to which we will all return tomorrow. This afternoon we are gathered as the church. We already know that you know what you are doing as fundraisers. What we want you to do is not to try to wow us with your presentation. We are sure that it is good and somebody spent a lot of time on it. We want you to simply have a conversation with us and listen to us. So would you please just turn that thing off and just talk with us?"

The president replied, "Well, uh, okay. What would you like to know?" Another person on the selection team said, "We would like to know who you are. We want to know the people with whom we will be entrusting this very important effort. We want to know why your presence among us will change us. So please sit down and just speak with us. We want to listen not to a presentation but to *you.* Your fundraising strategies and how your program will work for us are just details. First, we need to know who you are."

The New Baby Is a Witness

Hidden behind the clutter left by the collapse of the Constantinian synthesis, the church that too many people experience is only the marketing experience of the church, whether the marketing comes in the form of a deal, cause, or spiritual helps. Others may experience the church as some massive institution whose ways and structures are so foreign to their lives that the church itself cannot be encountered. And others may experience the church as representing some religion that is in competition with other religions. As the church struggles to be reborn, the church's prime and perhaps only task is to gift the world with who the church really is, bursting into our reality without any agenda other than the revelation of God afresh and new.

The birth of the church two thousand years ago was not the result of some marketing strategy. Nor was it an attempt to introduce a new religion into the world. There was not some master plan with a seven-step or five-point strategic vision to achieve certain programmatic objectives. There was no goal of building an institution that would vaunt some hierarchical structure and exercise power in the world.

The church was born out of the Spirit of God. Its purpose was to witness to the saving activity of God, not as proffering a deal, cause, or spiritual assistance but to be a transparent sign in which and through which Jesus is encountered, experienced, known, and lives. The church's relationship to Jesus is not simply to be identified with a historical person. The church's identification with Jesus is its DNA. Jesus not only gives the church its DNA. Jesus also *is* the church's DNA. Jesus abides or lives in the church (John 15:4 and others). Thus, Jesus can speak about his being "the vine" and the church being "the branches" (John 15:5). Vine and branch are of the same DNA. The church as the Body of Christ is more than just a metaphor. It is reality.

The work of religion professor Marianne Sawicki is helpful here. In her book *Seeing the Lord*, she discloses that the New Testament texts and the practices of the church were not to continue to report on what happened "back then" but that the texts and practices were ongoing descriptors or "specifications" of a crucified and risen Jesus who is available and accessible to the church and who continues to animate it.[1] Jesus, the being of the church, its practices, and its texts are all one. It's the same DNA. Thus, in the church's DNA is Jesus' solidarity with the world, his love for all creation, his radical inclusiveness and valuing of all, his preferential option for the poor, his healing compassion, his death as God's ultimate faithfulness to the world, his resurrection as triumph over the powers of sin and death, and the promised future over which he is Lord.

Both the Gospel of John and the composite story of Luke–Acts make it quite clear that the Spirit of God is the birthing life-force of the church. They disagree only in the details. In the former, the resurrected Jesus appears on Easter evening to his disciples in a room behind locked doors and visibly breathes on them the Holy Spirit (John 20:22). In Luke-Acts, the crucified and risen Jesus appears to his apostles, informs them of the coming outpouring of the Spirit (Luke 24:49; Acts 1:5), and departs from them (Luke 24:51; Acts 1:9). On the Day of Pentecost, God, as promised, unleashes the Holy Spirit upon the apostles (Acts 2:1-4). This Holy Spirit is the creative breath of God that in the beginning moved over the waters of chaos and created the "heavens and the earth" (Genesis 1:1). It is the same breath that the author of Genesis says God breathed into a lump of earth and created a living human being (2:7). It overshadowed and conceived in Mary the person of Jesus (Luke 1:35). It anointed Jesus in baptism and called him to his mission (Luke 4:18). It is this same breath of God that raised Jesus from the dead (Romans 1:4). God's creative, calling, and dead-raising Spirit is the Spirit that created the church and continues to breathe life into it. The life it breathes is the life of the crucified and risen Messiah.

As the introductory pages of this book stated, this is an exciting time to be the church. In this postmodern, post-

Constantinian, and perhaps soon-to-be post-denominational world, the church is in the process of being reborn. As midwives to this rebirth, let's be clear about what is coming out of the womb. The new baby is a witness.

The Church as Witness to the Resurrection

In Luke 24:48 and again in Acts 1:8, the author of Luke-Acts records Jesus saying to the apostles, "You will be my witnesses." The apostles would be the charter members of the church. This charge to them is not a simple reminder of what they saw and experienced with Jesus. Jesus is not saying, "You will be my *eye*-witnesses." He is saying, "You will be my *witnesses*." It is to confer onto them and thus the church the church's full identity and calling in the world. "Witness to the resurrection" is both what the church *is* and what the church *does.* It is the animation of its own DNA. Dogs bark. Cats purr. Salmon swim upstream to spawn. The church lives as "witness to the resurrection." An examination of the first chapter of Acts is helpful here.

As the eleven apostles gather in the waiting period between the ascension of Jesus and the receipt of the promised Holy Spirit, they come together to attend to the task of choosing a person to replace Judas. Judas is the one who betrayed Jesus and is now dead. It is important that the eleven become twelve again.[2] "Witness to the resurrection" becomes their self-understanding.

> "So one of the men who have accompanied us during all the time that the Lord Jesus went in and out among us, beginning from the baptism of John until the day he was taken up from us—one of these must become a *witness with us to his resurrection.*" (Acts 1:21-22 [emphasis mine])

In Peter's Pentecost sermon (Acts 2:14-36), a formula emerges that theologian Jürgen Moltmann identifies as the central statement of the church's primitive proclamation.[3] One might say that they are the first words of the newborn. "This Jesus, who was crucified, God has raised from the dead, and we are witnesses." This formula, or versions of it, punctuates sermons or speeches throughout Acts. In using this repetitive formula, the author wants to hold before the reader the notion that the activity of the apostles and thus the infant church is synonymous with their identity and calling as a "witness to the resurrection."

This symbol, "witness to the resurrection," in its biblical context, has the understanding of one who both verbally testifies to facts one knows to be true—"The crucified Jesus is raised from the dead"—and who is compelled to risk or give one's life fully for that truth because one has been seized by the power of the resurrection. What this means is that the witness—that is, the church—is owned, seized, compelled, motivated, driven, empowered, formed, and directed by the crucified and risen Jesus. Jesus is the life-force. The Holy Spirit breathes into the church this life-force and animates the church with the power of the death and resurrection of Jesus and its cosmic and future-rattling implications. The witnesses give themselves and risk all for this crucified and risen Jesus because they know that the story that has seized them is true. They abandon everything, including whatever story had previously owned them, to "witness" to the new reality.

There is no way to overemphasize the importance of the resurrection of Jesus from the dead. It is why we, the church, pay attention to Jesus. If Jesus is not raised from the dead, then Jesus is just another Jewish righteous sufferer—a martyr, so to speak. What the apostles encountered was not a Jesus who was resuscitated back to life, only to die again later. They encountered a Jesus raised beyond death. Death no longer has any power over him, and being beyond death, he can make unconditional promises. He holds power over the future. Because Jesus has been raised, nothing is the same anymore. The resurrection restructures everything.

To be a witness to the resurrection means to be grasped by the notion that God has already acted. God has already decided. God has done for us and to us what we are unable to do ourselves. There is nothing that we can do to assist God, add to what God has done, or to take credit for it. Nor can we play God with our deals, causes, or chaplaincy. All we can and must do is reorder our lives so that our life together is a living appropria-

Witness to the Resurrection:
An Identity and Calling Conferred

The biblical and theological freight of the term "witness to the resurrection" is enormous for the focus of this book and the reconception of an authentic church. So that the reader might be brought more fully into the meaning of this identity and calling, I want to briefly discuss here this symbol and implications for the self-understanding of the church. Although "witness to the resurrection" is peppered throughout Luke-Acts, three key passages get at the heart of its meaning: (1) Jesus' words to his apostles, "You are witnesses of these things" (Luke 24:48); (2) Jesus again speaking to the apostles, "You will be my witnesses" (Acts 1:8); and (3) the identity and calling of the church expressed in the choosing of the replacement twelfth apostle, "a witness with us to his resurrection" (Acts 1:22).

In each of the three passages and throughout Luke-Acts (as well as in John and other New Testament texts), the word *witness* comes from the same root from which we get the word *martyr*. Even though we have a rich heritage of martyrdom in the church, it would be a mistake to reduce this word in these ancient texts to the meaning of a suffering "victim" to whom an injustice was done. *Witness* in this context is a wieldy and wholly positive identity. The witness knows and testifies to the truth; yet, the testimony of the witness is much more than words. The witness's life, risked and given for the sake of the truth, is the primary testimony.

In the three passages, "these things," "my," and "his resurrection" are joined to the word *witness* through the use of the genitive case. In biblical Greek, the genitive case is a multifaceted construct, carrying a variety of nuances. In the case of these three passages, the construct is arguably both a possessive and subjective genitive. As a possessive, this means that "these things," "my," and "his resurrection" own the witness. The witness is now possessed by the resurrection of Jesus from the dead! As a subjective genitive, "these things," "my," and "his resurrection" are subject over the witnessing activity of the witness. They birth, define, and animate the witness. They speak to the witness in the delivery room. They speak to and shape the witness as the witness develops and lives. They are the witness's fuel. The "witness to the resurrection," then, does not just have the right information or facts. The "witness to the resurrection" is transformed and driven by what has happened—the crucified Jesus raised from the dead.

tion that is true to the news of what God has done, continues to do, and the future God has disclosed and will give to us. We are witnesses.

Witness and Jesus

It is helpful to remember that the author of Luke and Acts is both a historian and a theologian and has an agenda of giving an "orderly account" (Luke 1:3). His orderly account is going to score theological and ecclesiological points. An examination of the book of Acts thus discloses that the author posits an infant church that looks, thinks, imagines, and acts like Jesus. Much of the book of Acts seems like a replication of the Gospel of Luke, except the church, in the persons of the apostles, has seemingly replaced Jesus as the subject of the narratives. With Jesus as its DNA, the church functions as the continuation of Jesus in the world.

The previous chapter of this book closed with the assertion that the rebirthing of the church means that we give people not propositions, deals, and such, but that we give people Jesus. We see this assertion at work in Acts. After reporting the outpouring of the Holy Spirit, Peter's evangelical sermon to the crowd assembled in Jerusalem, and the birth of the church, Acts 2 con-

The Resurrection Changes Everything
Walter R. Bouman[4]

The gospel tradition locates the basis for Jesus' authority in his claims to be the eschatological messiah because the starting point and content of the good news proclaimed by Jesus' earliest disciples is the simple statement that Jesus has been raised from the dead (Rom. 1:4, Acts 2:24, etc.). What the followers of Jesus experienced when they were encountered by Jesus after his execution and burial was not his resuscitation. That would have meant that Jesus returned to the same mode of existence that was his prior to death, that he had resumed his life where it had left off, that his eventual death had merely been postponed. That was indeed the expectation of many pious Jews, that righteous martyrs, unjustly deprived of the fullness of life, would return to live an appropriate length of days. What the disciples encountered was infinitely more awesome. If it were true that Jesus was crucified because of his messianic claims, then his execution represented a judgment upon those claims and the claims of his eschatological authority. His resurrection was an eschatological reversal of that judgment. Jesus had been raised to the "eschaton," to the final future of the reign of God. That is the significance of his appearances and disappearances that are no longer subject to "this age," the age of death. That is finally the significance of Luke's "ascension" narratives. Jesus does not leave the world and go to some "place" outside of the cosmos. He ascends into the eschatological future, and he is therefore not "gone." For he is present with and to his disciples with the power of the future. The Acts of the Apostles is not the story of the community *after* Jesus, but rather the story of the community *under* Jesus.

Now the disciples were required to radically re-envision the future. The messianic age had begun. They

had seen the outcome of history proleptically, in pre-
view, in the midst of history. They now knew that the
future belonged to Jesus and no other. He could make
unconditional promises, promises no longer conditioned
by death. In his resurrection the eschatological future
was disclosed, the "secret of the ages" that the Kingdom
of God would triumph over the power of death. Life, not
death would have the last word. The Gospel of Matthew
could thus conclude with the ultimate claim of the risen
Christ. "All authority in heaven and earth has been given to
me." The disciples are sent with that eschatological authority and they receive Jesus' final promise: "I am with you
always until the end of the present age" (Matt. 20:16-20).

To be grasped by such an event changed the life of
the disciple community. They had eschatological authority, the authority of the Holy Spirit, the "down payment"
of the messianic age (Eph. 1:13-14) which enabled them
to live in the house of the future as if it were already
their own. They were freed to be the community that
anticipated the age to come because it had already begun. That changed their participation in history, and
therefore set in motion changes in history itself.

cludes with a description of the church's life together and its
ingathering of more people (2:42-47). Acts 3 opens with a specific story of the church as witness in the world. Peter and John
are going up to the temple, where they encounter a man at the
gate who has been lame from birth and daily is carried to this
place. As he sees Peter and John walk up, he asks them "for alms"
(3:3). Their encounter with this man is illustrative of the witness
of the infant church and the witness of the authentic church God
is today summoning to life through rebirth: the lame man is a
consumer (which is not to demean the long-time suffering of
this man, his deep needs, nor the sincerity of his request). He
comes to the temple to beg each day. He is also a victim. He is
stuck in his own story. He wears his lameness as his identity. He
can not imagine any other existence.

Peter and John will not allow him to remain a victim. They also do not succumb to his consumer needs. They will not give him "silver or gold" (3:6). They propose no deal, no cause, and give no spiritual advice. They do not have a three-step program up their sleeves. They give him what they had to give as the church: they give him Jesus (3:6). The man stands up and walks. No longer a victim, he is in the temple dancing around and praising God (3:9). He has a new story, or better yet, a new story *has* him. He is a witness. As chapters three and four unfold, this man's adoption of a new story and the witness of Peter and John do not happen without peril; yet, as others try to attack and deconstruct the new story and reality out of which they live—the crucified and risen Jesus as Lord and Messiah—the story holds them. It is not because they are especially brave, bold, or smart. It is because of the tenacity and bold truth of the story in the power of Holy Spirit. After all, they are just "uneducated and ordinary men" (4:13).

The rest of the book of Acts discloses the same pattern as this episode at the temple. The apostles, empowered by the Holy Spirit and grasped by the crucified and living Jesus, encounter a world that is simultaneously open and hostile to their story. Some experience their witness and are drawn into their expanding church with great joy and hope. Others experience their witness as a huge threat, hold them in contempt, and want to kill the story and them. Yet, as the book of Acts unfolds with the witness of the infant church, we see Jesus. We see Jesus in the person of Stephen as he faces his accusers and suffers an awful execution (6:8–7:60). Not willing to abandon his witness, he was powerfully held by the Holy Spirit, saw his future, recognized the presence of Jesus, and courageously died, praying for his executioners. The martyrdom of Stephen made such an impression on the author of Acts that the author's account seems like a conspicuous replication of the trial and crucifixion of Jesus.

We see Jesus in the persons of Peter, Philip, and Paul as they reach out and include Gentiles into the new community, many of whom (such as Cornelius, the Roman centurion) represent

everything that the other people being gathered into the fledg-
ling new church had formerly been taught to hate and de-
spise. But there is a new day with a new story.

We see Jesus in the person of Paul, whose mission will
not be thwarted by shipwrecks, imprisonment, lack of funds,
or threats of death. In the person of Paul we see the church in
action on a ship out on high, stormy, and dangerous seas near
Malta. Paul is actually a prisoner to the soldiers on board the
ship, but in the midst of the storms, Paul assures the men
that they will be safe. After assuring their safety, he takes bread,
gives thanks to God, breaks it, and feeds himself and the others (Acts 27:35ff.). It is a metaphor for the church today, gathering in the midst of a culture that does not understand it and
in the midst of storms that threaten and rock both the church
and the culture. As a trusted mentor once said to me, "When
you don't know what to say or do in a time of crisis, you can
always gather folks together and shove bread and wine in their
mouths." Paul said it this way: "For as often as you eat this
bread and drink the cup, you proclaim the Lord's death until
he comes" (1 Corinthians 11:26). That's right. It is not the
story of the current confusion, crisis, or consternation that is
going to have the last word. Nor is it the next strategic plan,
deal, or cause. It is the story of the crucified and risen Lord, to
whom the future belongs, who tenaciously holds the church,
and who will have the final word.

The journey into the world of the book of Acts that has
unfolded in these pages is not an attempt to glamorize the
infant church or to lay the groundwork to replicate it. As the
opening discussion in this book suggested, it is in the infant
church where we might find clues that serve to reconceive an
authentic church today. Everything we need for the rebirthing
and reconstruction of the church is already in our inventory.
If we look closely at the theological grounding and relational
constructs of the infant church community, we will see life-
giving material that we must allow to guide our imagination
today.

A True Community with a True Story: Glimpses into the Infant Church

The people of the infant church in essence understood themselves to be both the embodiment and the continuation of the crucified and risen Christ in the world. As such, they lived as a contrast society. The world had one story. They lived out of another and organized their life together as a witness to their story. The story was their currency. Their witness included both investments in protecting the integrity of the story and the appropriation of their lives as consistent with the claims of the story. Their relationship to the story was thus dialectic. The story shaped their life together, and their life together reflected and solidified the integrity of the story.

As a window into the life of the infant church, the work of Yale professor Wayne Meeks, in his book *The First Urban Christians*, is especially helpful here.[5] Using the Pauline corpus in the New Testament and other first-century texts, Meeks is able to put together a portrait of the life of the infant church. As one enters into the world of the infant church, one will see that some of the kinds of things that occupy the church's imagination today are not in any way at stake in the early church. Recruitment of members, designing new programs, rescuing people from hell, enlisting people in causes, and providing spiritual self-helps to accommodate cultural lifestyles are not concepts within the world of the infant church. What is at stake in the infant church and how it is ordered is authenticity—being who they understand themselves to be.

One of the issues that Meeks takes on is the claim made by some of the earliest people to attack Christianity. Attempting to discredit, they claimed that the first Christians came from the most illiterate and lowest class of people.[6] Meeks's textual evidence concludes that such a claim is a lie.[7] Christianity was also not some Marxist-like movement among the proletariat. The social fabric of the infant church was essentially middle class. There were certainly people of poverty involved, and there were people of wealth, both men and

women. The social status of the first Christians—determined
by profession or trade, ethnicity, family reputation, urban or
rural location, ability to read or write, and other consider-
ations of more than wealth—discloses that they were neither
a powerful group nor a collectively oppressed group. As the
title of Meeks' book suggests, the people who made up the
first two decades of the infant church "generally reflected a
fair cross-section of the urban society."[8] It's the same today.
The church is made up of all kinds of folks.

The *Ekklesia*

The *ekklesia* (the Greek term that is translated "church" in En-
glish-language Bibles) was a unique social structure within the
Greco-Roman world. It did not align precisely with existing
models of household groups, volunteer organizations, the syna-
gogue, or the philosophical or rhetoric schools of the day. Although it disclosed a certain affinity with some of these groups,
it had its own particular essence.[9] The boundaries of the *ekklesia*
were not about place but about their own identity and calling.
So the *ekklesia* of the first two decades of the church were not
like extreme separatist groups, such as the Essenes who with-
drew in isolation to their own place. Members of the *ekklesia*
lived and interacted with other citizens in their neighborhoods,
workplaces, streets, and shops—again, like members of congregations do today. They also understood themselves to belong
not just to one group in one particular city but to the whole
collection of *ekklesia* groups in the empire. They sensed that they
belonged to a universal people of God. Letters, exchanges of vis-
its, and collections from among the groups served to reinforce
their collective identity and solidarity.[10]

  The rhetoric of the *ekklesia*, as illustrated in the letters of Paul,
carried both the sense of the sharp boundaries between them
and the social world around them and a very strong intimacy of
belonging. The Pauline letters are filled with expressions such as
"elect," "saints," "holy ones," "calling," "in Christ," "beloved,"
brothers," "sisters," "greet the brothers with a kiss," and "body
of Christ."

Baptism. Baptism was not only the initiation rite into the *ekklesia;* the ritual itself served to dramatize the break with "the world." The rhetoric—"baptized into Christ," "put on Christ," "into one body," "new creation," and "spirit of adoption"—portrays what a modern sociologist might call "the resocialization of conversion."[11] Three aspects about baptism into the *ekklesia* need to be lifted up here. The first is that in the ritual itself, the newly baptized would give an ecstatic response, "Abba! Father!" The ecstatic cry is a sign that the baptized has received the "gift of the Spirit" and "sonship" (see Galatians 3:26–4:6 and Romans 8:15-17). "Sonship" means "incorporating the person into the one Son of God."[12] The baptized has now become a "witness." The story of the church has become the person's story, not as information but as transformation. The story owns, defines, and empowers the baptized.

The second aspect about baptism into the *ekklesia* that is important here is that the initiates actually stripped off their clothing and were baptized naked. (Try that today and see what happens!) The ritual concluded with the new initiate putting on new clothing. This visual and concrete imagery illuminated the distinct break from the past and the world's story and the emergence of a "new creation" that has "put on Christ."

The third aspect is that the ritual carried with it staying power. Because the ritual was as much an initiation into an ongoing story as it was an event, baptism was to be constantly recalled and revisited as clarification of identity and calling. Integral to this identity and calling was the metaphor, "dying and rising." Baptism "into the death" of Christ and being "raised to new life" (cf. Romans 3:3-11) was the fullest expression of that metaphor, and the metaphor became grafted into the DNA of the church's story. It gave content and hope to suffering, persecution, and the daily struggles to live authentically the Christian life to which the church and its members are called.[13]

As we seek to rebirth an authentic church in today's postmodern, post-Constantinian, and consumer culture, perhaps a recovery of the radical claims of baptism might be a starting place. The syrupy sentimentality connected with baptism today was totally foreign to the practices of the infant church. This means, for instance, that churches that practice infant baptism may need to reexamine their practices. This is not to discount that baptism in its essence is the visible adoption of the baptized into the church's story; the transformational power in the authenticity of the story is that baptism is not about us or our choices. It's about God and God's choice. This book has argued exhaustively against any kind of deal or personal decision associated with the truth of the church's good news. God does it all, and the ritual of an infant being baptized, who has no clue or no choice in the matter, perfectly expresses the gospel. It is a witness to the resurrection.

On the other hand, do the radical claims of baptism live in the consciousness of the baptized? The evidence points against that. Parents often do not keep the promises they made at the font to raise their child in the church. Sponsors or godparents often do little more than stand by the font and show up at the party afterwards. People also make promises and some time later decide to leave the church. And adult classes on baptism have little appeal. Few people are going to give up Monday-night football, an evening to relax at home, or much of their discretionary time to attend a baptism class. At my congregation, we hold monthly hour-long baptism seminars required of all adults wishing to have their child baptized. Adults, deciding to be baptized themselves, need to go through our whole new-member process. About 50 percent of the time at the seminars, one of the parents does not come. The baptismal sponsors rarely come. Given the questions that the parents ask, most of the discussion focuses on the technical aspects. Twenty minutes, at best, are spent on the actual theology and adaptive challenges of baptism. This is not a problem only I experience; it is also a problem among pastors of differing church affiliations. It is not at all uncommon for a couple to go down the street to the Methodist congregation because they thought that we require too many hoops for them to jump through. It is also not uncommon for a couple to present themselves to my congregation because they thought another congregation was too "rigid."

A wonderful visual that works in my congregation to bring focus to the claims of baptism is that we have a huge baptismal font with flowing water in our worship space around which we preach, teach, and lead worship. Attention is frequently drawn to it. The frequency with which I see people dipping their fingers in it and making the sign of the cross on their foreheads tells me that perhaps more and more are "getting it."

What would be the effect if there were a concentrated effort to recover the identity and calling of baptism as belonging to the church and being "in Christ"? What would be the effect in corporate boardrooms, in the mechanic's shop, at soccer practice, or in divorce court if those who are baptized were consciously aware that they are the church and therefore "in Christ"? What difference would it make in the person who has been deeply wronged and injured by a co-worker, family member, or in-law? What difference would it make when the doctor tells you there is "nothing more that can be done?" What difference would it make with a tough decision you have to make at the office tomorrow?

Worship. Though the term *ekklesia* would define a unique social construct within the ancient world, it first meant literally an assembly of people, called out of the world and into a special gathering for worship. The worship was not to just any god. The worship was to the God who is made known through Jesus the Christ.

The coming together was a regular occurrence. The writings of Justin Martyr reveal that by about 150 C.E., the coming together was weekly—on Sunday, the day of the resurrection.[14] An examination of what they did when they came together discloses that very early on a liturgy developed. They did not come to be entertained, get some helpful information, or have their individual consumer needs met. Worship was not one of several programs the church offered. Worship was simply what the *ekklesia* did as a matter of its identity and calling. There was "a hymn, a lesson, a revelation, a tongue, or an interpretation" (1 Corinthians 14:26). Philippians 2:6 was probably an early hymn. The liturgy was for the purposes of "building up" (cf. 1 Corinthians 14:26).

The "building up" had to do with the construction of a "community ethos,"[15] or cultural architecture, as this book has discussed. Regular readings and homilies were part of the liturgy. There was some teaching or exhortation, the nature of which we see in the paraenetic (or ethics) sections of the letters of Paul. And, of course, there were prayers. "In the name of Jesus" or some other similar formulae peppered the speech in the assembly. Though there seemed to be a "charismatic and free" character to the gatherings, they were "marked by these forms."[16]

Worship, then, had no other agenda than to attend to the church's identity and calling. Worship was its primary witness. In worship all the components of the church's story came together. Because they gathered for worship not in a vacuum but in the midst of a world that was hostile to the church and owned by another story, the gathered community's character was forged. Jesus, the one who was crucified, had been raised from the dead. The church was joined to him. Nothing could alter or change that. This is not to say that conflict, division, fighting, and rigorous theological debate did not exist within the church. The scriptures (cf. the Corinthian correspondence) and early church history clearly testify to the church's difficulties. Yet soaking in much of the rhetoric of the letters of Paul and the church's scriptures, one gets the clear impression that these gatherings were filled with much gratitude, joy, humility, love, and hope.

The Eucharist. Along with baptism, the Eucharist was the other "major ritual complex" that happened when the *ekklesia* came together.[17] Like baptism, it was a boundary-setting ritual, reinforcing their identity and calling. The words "one bread," "one body," "one Lord," and the like reinforced their cohesion. Coming together also reminded them that they lived in a world where people were hungry (see 1 Corinthians 11). The most important aspect of the meal was that it embodied the essential story that owns the church, its DNA, and thus Christ. In the meal is God's faithfulness to the world—even unto the "night in which our Lord Jesus was betrayed" that led to a cross, to an empty tomb, and to steadfast hope in the future. Hearing the words "the body of Christ given for you" and "the blood of Christ shed for you" is not helpful information. It is transformation.

The prevalence of fertile eucharistic imagery imbedded in the texts of the New Testament, the rich stories of meals that define the identity of the people of God in the Hebrew scriptures, and the core importance of the meal in the early gatherings of the infant church must cause us to question the reasons why many congregations do not routinely share the Eucharist when they gather for worship. The Eucharist builds authentic cultural architecture, not as a tactic or strategy but because the Eucharist *is* the church's story. This is not to devalue those traditions in which the Eucharist is not routinely shared but rather to raise the reality that congregations whose traditions may indeed strongly emphasize routine sharing of the Eucharist do not actually do that. Many congregations choose not to have the Eucharist regularly because of the time it takes or because it is "too mysterious." The logic is that people doing church shopping will be turned off if the service runs long, and they probably will not understand the ritual anyhow. Moreover, the ritual has a lot of baggage attached it. It reminds some of the excesses and corruption of the medieval Roman Catholic Church: "We do not want a lot of chancel prancing in our church!" It also reminds people of how divided the church is these days. Some congregations practice closed communion: "You can only participate if you are one of us." Because of that practice, the message inadvertently carries over into other congregations. People get confused, thinking, "Am I allowed to participate or not?" The feeling of many is that it is better to have Holy Communion less frequently than have to deal with all the baggage, contradictions, and market-driven issues.

From the Delivery Room

Entering into the world of the infant church gives us clues to the rebirthing of the church. It also gives us much hope. Though a great chasm separates our twenty-first-century North American world from the first-century Greco-Roman-Palestinian world of the infant church, the womb in the delivery room is the same. Everything we need for the rebirthing of the church is there in the rich soil of the church's ancient and authentic story. The texts are there. The rituals are there. The hope is there. The building blocks are not dead, because the one who is embodied in the DNA is not dead either. He lives. He is risen.

Can we break with consumer- and market-driven thinking to reimagine the church? Can we set aside all the baggage from the Constantinian hangover—the deals, the causes, and the spiritual needs to support today's lifestyles—and name the essential facets of an authentic church? While finishing up the manuscript for this book, I was called into a congregation to provide some guidance in helping them resolve what seemed like a monstrous conflict. This congregation had experienced rapid growth in one of our country's fastest-growing areas. It was blessed with talent, faith, and courage among its paid staff and among its unpaid leaders. No one knows how the conflict got started but they were all entangled and misbehaving in a very unhealthy conflict over a new vision, a change of staff roles, opening a second campus, evangelism strategies, worship, stewardship, and just about anything else you might want to name. In talking with one of the key leaders, I asked the question, "What do you see as the problem and the solution?" The problem was described as complex, the solution evasive and no doubt multi-tiered. The matter was seen as being so complicated that it defied simple answers. I became frustrated myself and without any forethought blurted out, "It's just church."

It really is "just church." Like the conflict at the congregation I described, it is difficult to name exactly how the church got to the shape that it is in and how the renewal of the church and its congregations has become so complicated. Parts of this book have attempted to diagnose "the crisis." A lot of blame has been laid at Constantine's feet. But the reality is that it *is* "just church." We have a story about a wonderfully magnificent and gracious God who is in love with the people this God created, people who are inappropriate and broken in multiple ways. We have a community in which and through which this story lives, calls, and transforms. It's just church.

Chapter Five

Intentional Cultural Architecture

I once heard a pediatrician speak at a gathering of parents and make this startling statement: "It is a shame that the laws of the world in which we live do not allow us to give birth to our first child, raise her to the age of six or so, learn from all the mistakes that we have made, throw the child away, and then start for real with the family we want to raise." This tongue-in-cheek statement from the good doctor brought an immediate collective belly laugh from the audience because we all recognized the steep learning curve of being a parent. I know many people who feel the same way about the church—that it would be a lot easier to simply start all over again. Of course, we can no more throw away the church than we can throw away a beloved child of our own, no matter the number of mistakes we have made. The task before us, therefore, is to join the church in an adaptive movement that transforms it into the God-driven, authentic organism originally birthed by the Spirit that lives and breathes "in Christ."

Envisioning an Authentic Church

Vision is the ability to see things not as they are but as they can be. The task of congregations today who desire to break out of the Constantinian hangover and to be the transformational movement birthed by God's Spirit is first to see alternative ways of being. In chapter one, I introduced a chart that began to name essential aspects of the church that live in tension with one another in today's culture. This table appears again on the following page. In the left column, I attempt to describe the self-understanding of ecclesiological concepts inherent to a consumer-driven, technical-in-approach church that derives much of its being from the effects of the Constantinian synthesis. The right column attempts to reach into the womb of the fertile soil of the infant church and raise up something altogether different. It is a vision, purporting to be authentic and God-driven, that would inherently have transformational and adaptive traction in our consumer culture.

The Church and Membership

Much of this book has been devoted to the essence of the church and thus the meaning of belonging to the church. We do not *go* to church. We do not belong *to* a church. We *are* the church. The church is not its building, programs, or services. It's the people. It's not an institution. It is an organic movement. The existence of the people and the life of this organic movement together are a witness.

I once had a congregational member who rarely came to worship and who sent in a small check at the end of the year with a small note that read, "Here are my dues for the year." American Express used to have a marketing slogan to hype the unique opportunity of owning one of their credit cards. It said, "Membership has its privileges." In the envisioning of an authentic congregation for today, we must deconstruct all consumer notions of membership. If one understands membership from a technical aspect, then to be a member means to be a beneficiary of whatever it is that the church offers. One will simply have to do the minimum requirement necessary to stay on the congregation's rolls. If one understands that membership is to be counted among those on an adaptive journey—a journey from being owned by one story to being owned by another—then one

Table 1
Cultural Architecture for an Authentic Transformational Church

FROM	TO
• The church inherited from Constantine	• Authentic
• Technical in Approach	• Adaptive Transformation
• Consumer-driven	• God-driven

The Church

• Institution to which people might belong	• A movement of people "in Christ"
• Offers deals for salvation	• Exists as a witness to the new reality and its promised future as disclosed in the ancient and authentic story of the life, death and resurrection of Jesus Christ
• Takes up causes that benefit the community and world	
• Serves as a chaplain offering spiritual services and programs	
	• A contrast community

The Meaning of Membership

• Membership	• Partnership and ownership
• Could be necessary for salvation	• Membership itself is a witness to the new reality and the promised future
• Fitting God into "my" story	
• Insures having "my" needs met	• Surrenders self to God's story
	• Is called to meet God's needs

The Role of the Pastors and Staff

• Pastors and staff serve as chaplains to meet needs	• Pastors and staff serve as stewards of the church's story
• Dispensers of programs and service	• They provide transformational, adaptive servant-leadership
• They "run" the church	• They build up and equip all to own the church's identity and calling
• Members of the "clergy club" have higher authority and power than "the laity"	
	• They bow down to their calling and lift others up to fulfill the mission

Baptism

• A deal to escape damnation	• Initiation into the church as a contrast community
• One of the services the church offers	• Confers identity and calling

is going to give one's self to the full expression of the body. As we move deeper into twenty-first century, it should be no surprise that more and more congregations are paying attention to average weekly worship attendance as the primary marker determining their size than to the total number on their membership rolls. Total membership is a meaningless number. The church—the *ekklesia*—is who shows up, not who belongs.

Concerning Pastors and Certified Church Professionals

Much of the hope for the rebirthing of the church lies in the quality and passions of many of the people who are called into ordained ministry or some form of ministry that the church often calls "professional laity." Many of my colleagues in ministry are among some of the most talented and dedicated servant-leaders I know. They are inspirational witnesses in who they are and how they conduct their lives. They build up people around them and exude confidence and trust in the body they serve. Unfortunately, not all are that way. Many of the difficulties the church faces today lie not only at the feet of Constantine. They lie also at the feet of the church's rostered leaders—the "clergy." When I use "clergy" here, I am referring both to the ordained and those given professional credentials in other ways ("Associates in Ministry" in the ELCA, "Certified Lay Professionals" in the Presbyterian Church [USA], "Deacons" in other expressions, and the like).

The problems many clergy cause are not fully their fault. They were trained in theological seminaries that taught them to serve a church in a culture which no longer exists. Moreover, the training many received was mainly technical. They were shaped to be chaplains and not transformational leaders. And in an age where larger churches are becoming more prevalent, few were trained to serve in a multistaff ministry or to lead such a staff. Those who teach in seminaries were not trained for today's challenges, nor were most of the bishops or other such people who are called to administer judicatories or clusters of congregations.

Whether we like it or not, most of us belong to congregations and church bodies in which the clergy hold enormous
power. The systems of most church bodies reinforce a special
sense of privilege and entitlement among the clergy. Systems and
church polity, invented by clergy, make it extremely difficult to
remove a member of the clergy from a congregation. Let a minister of music fall in disfavor with a congregation and be asked
to leave, and that person will usually be lucky to get any kind of
severance other than the absolute minimum. Not so with clergy.
Removing clergy, whether for misconduct or for reasons of a lack
of fit with the congregation's mission, is rarely done without a
high cost and lots of pain to all involved. This is not to say that
there are not those clergy who make enormous sacrifices, may
earn substandard wages without complaining, serve with great
attitudes and passion, and know when it is time for them to love
a congregation by leaving it. But the reality is that clergy, in general, carry a special sense of power. And all too often, the laity
work to give clergy their power. How many times have you seen
a team of talented, successful people gather for a meeting with a
member of the clergy and immediately defer to the clergyperson?
Is not the clergyperson expected to have special knowledge and
authority on almost all matters?

In the early 1980s a construction company was building a
number of identical prefabricated buildings in the Middle East.
Early on, it discovered that it was losing lots of money on its
labor costs. Each building crew consisted of a European supervisor and skilled laborers from the Philippines. No amount of
additional incentives or new tactics could change the trends. Each
building was taking much longer to construct than estimated,
and there were many problems with the quality. After studying
the situation, an idea arose. It was decided that certain crews of
Filipinos would be unleashed on a new site without there being
a European supervisor. The results of this idea were staggering.
The buildings were completed at almost half the previous labor
costs and in half the time. The quality was outstanding, and everybody seemed to be much happier. It was a new day. What was
discovered was that the Filipinos had been sociologically and

culturally conditioned to always defer to the "white man." In the presence of the "white man," the Filipinos turned off their thinking and creative skills and simply followed instructions. When unleashed on a project on their own, they flourished. They worked as a team. They were out from under the weight of the presence of the "white man."

How many churches work like the portrait of this company when the Filipinos were subject to the "white man"? How many clergy function like the "white man"? What all does your pastor do? Make all the hospital calls? Lead all the prayers? Preside over most meetings? Control most decisions? Micro-manage all the details? If the answer is yes, then ask the question, Why? Essential to the authentic church is the full ownership of its identity and calling by all, not just the clergy. The fewer ministries the clergy do in your congregation, the more passionate and vital your congregation will be. The fewer ministries the clergy do the more effective and vibrant they will be in their own unique gift to the church and to the specific witness of their call.

Every Christian receives a call to ministry when he or she is baptized. Pastors receive a particular and important call: they are called to be stewards of the church's treasure—the gospel. They are to come to the table with theological and biblical authority earned through the sacrifices they make to keep themselves immersed in theological and biblical study, praxis, and reflection. If they happen to bring to the table some leadership skills, it's a bonus. It is the same with those called to specialized ministries. Clergy are called to "equip" (Ephesians 4:12) the people for ministry. For the clergy reading this book, please know that this is a new day. If you are not gifted or trained in empowerment servant-leadership, then pay the price to learn it. There are a number of great books and seminars that can equip you. If you are really serious, find a mentor who does this critical aspect of church leadership well. That's a biblical approach: Silas and Timothy had Paul; Joshua had Moses; Ruth had Naomi.

If you are not a member of the clergy but rather a member of the laity in your congregation, then insist that your pastor and other clergy do whatever it takes to be empowerment, permission-giving servant-leaders. What is at stake is whether your congregation will remain more like a Constantinian-bred institution or become a vibrant organic movement in which all own and are true partners in the congregation's life and mission.

Finally on this discussion, congregations need to find new vocabularies with which to describe the various people and their roles. Continued use of the words *clergy* and *lay* only serve to reinforce a hierarchical system. The word *volunteer* also needs to be exorcised from our vocabulary. The church does not *have* volunteers. Volunteers *are* the church. Until someone comes along with a better idea, I like the words that congregational leadership specialist Bill Easum uses: he speaks of people as being "paid servants" and "unpaid servants."

Transforming a congregation from being clergy dominated to a congregation where people are trusted and empowered to own the ministry will be an adaptive process that will require focused and consistent attention; however, congregations who have made this move have experienced amazing transformation.

More about Baptism

Designers of church buildings and worship centers, especially those identified with liturgical churches, almost always advocate for the baptismal font to be located at the entrance to the worship space. This seems to be the liturgical purist's point of view. Locating the font at the entrance emphasizes the ritual as the community's initiation rite. In today's culture and with the importance of the recovery of baptism as *prima facie* witness to the resurrection, perhaps it is better to locate the baptismal font in an area that can be easily seen by all the gathered worshipers. Instead of the birdbath-like fonts that sit in many worship spaces, the font may need to be as big and filled with as much water as practically possible. Really, it ought to be big enough for an adult to be put in it, and if the water can be flowing, moving, or falling in any way, all the better! In this postmodern world people are seized more by images than by words. You might be thinking that this is only a technical suggestion, but raising baptismal identity in the consciousness of the church so that it actually has traction in their lives is an adaptive process. The more attention that can be drawn to the ritual through preaching, teaching, and splashing lots of water the better.

Another approach to amplifying and using the transformational essence of this ritual relates to the use of baptismal sponsors (more often called godparents in many traditions). In addition to the sponsors selected by the baptized, which are invariably family members or friends, the congregation might also want to lift up and provide its own sponsors. These people would be those who are passionate about being faith mentors and willing to participate in ongoing empowerment and training so that they can fulfill their responsibilities. They would then invest themselves in the families and people they sponsored so that their baptismal identity and calling might grow and flourish within them. If the sponsors the family selected also want to undergo training to own more fully their identity as sponsors, then, by all means, include them too!

Worship

Nothing in the church's life creates more controversy and at the same time holds the greatest power for transformation than worship. Attention is here drawn to Table II on the following page. This table is a continuation of the adaptive moves introduced in Table I that are necessary for the envisioning and creation of congregational architecture for an authentic church. In an authentic church, worship is not a program. It is not even the church's main program. It is the essential and purest witness of the church. It's the primal expression of its being. It is what the church does. The event itself is transformational. Because the gospel happens when the church gathers, the community and individuals are changed. God goes to work on them. As Paul writes in Romans 1:16, the gospel is God's "power" (translated from *dunamis,* from which we get the word *dynamite*) to effect salvation. When salvation is understood in its fullest sense, not just to refer to one's hope beyond death but to a change in one's present state of being, the gospel and thus worship are transformational in the here and now. By "being saved," we are set free

Table II
Cultural Architecture for an Authentic Transformational Church

FROM	TO
• The church inherited from Constantine	• Authentic
• Technical in Approach	• Adaptive Transformation
• Consumer-driven	• God-driven

Worship

• The church's main program	• The community's essential witness to the resurrection
• Regular attendance may be necessary for eternal salvation	• The purist DNA of the church
• Attendees are an audience	• Liturgy as substance; it is witness
• Designed to meet different needs and tastes	• Shaped to give fullest witness that is indigenous to the culture
• Liturgy is one style among many	• Authentic in every way
• Best if it's an escape and uplifting	

Eucharist

• Individual deal with God to get sins forgiven	• Essential witness to the resurrection
• A mysterious memorial that remembers something that happened long ago	• Participation in the new age and future offered and promised by God
• May extend the length of the service	• The crucified and risen Christ as the gospel is present in the meal
• Can be divisive	• Radically inclusive

Discipleship

• Proof that one is saved	• Witness to the resurrection in one's life
• Disciplines that one must do	• Stewardship of one's life
• Standing on one's beliefs	• Going and serving where Jesus goes
• Providing something "meaningful" to do	• Strengthening one's witness

Ministries of Youth, Education, Fellowship, and Other

• Programs to meet people's needs	• Serves the witness of the church
• Owned primarily by clergy	• Owned by all the people

from whatever enslaves us. We are given space from whatever
threatens us. We are made well and whole. Our spirits are healed.
Cynicism gives way to hope. Doubt gives way to faith. Hatred
and bitterness are transformed into love. Fear is transformed into
faith. Cowardice gives way to courage. Theologically speaking,
when the gospel happens to us, we are grasped by God's
eschatological future. Nothing has changed, but everything has
changed. All is right.

The Importance of Liturgy. Say the words "liturgical church" to
many in today's world and they may not have a clue what you
are saying. For others, the word *liturgical* may conjure up images
of a stodgy, deeply traditional, and institutional experience with
rituals and rites that are often unintelligible and reek of power
and authority. To offer a corrective here to these images, *liturgy*
literally means "the work of the people." Liturgy in this discussion is simply definitive of worship in which all the gathered
people participate and own, including the Eucharist.

Many congregations who claim to have liturgical worship
are not liturgical at all. They confuse liturgical to mean that the
ordained and the chancel appointments wear vestments, aco-
lytes wear robes, the church follows a lectionary, and that much
of the words of the service are chanted or intoned. Yet at these
congregations, the ordained might lead the entire service. Children might be excluded from the Eucharist because they have
not been confirmed or have not yet undergone some sort of training that earns them the right to receive communion. Visitors
might be unable to participate because much of the music seems
odd and strange. Such worship is not liturgical because it is not
fully participatory.

On the other hand, there are those congregations who take pride
in not being "liturgical." The pastor wears no vestments at all. The
choir does most of the singing, and it feels more like entertainment
than worship. The congregation generally sits in a nonparticipatory
posture like an audience at a play. The highlight of the gathering is
perhaps the pastor standing up and giving a forty-minute sermon.
These congregations are indeed not liturgical.

In a true liturgical church, the ordained minister might only preach, preside at baptisms, and serve as celebrant for the Eucharist. Everything else might be done by the people—from leading pieces of the service, reading the scriptures, welcoming people and making announcements, leading the congregation in prayer, serving bread and wine from the table, assisting with baptisms, giving testimonials, leading children's messages, and, when worship has concluded, taking elements from the table to the hospitalized and homebound so as to include them in the Eucharist. From time to time, it might even be appropriate for a nonordained person to preside at baptisms and celebrate the Eucharist. When the pastor is away, it is perhaps better for a pastoral intern under the pastor's supervision or perhaps the president of the congregation to preside over these rituals rather than having some outside but officially "ordained" person come in and do them. To insist that only the ordained can do certain things, no matter what the circumstances are, is very Constantinian. It is not the person who presides who gives the baptism or the meal its authority. The authority is inherent in the ritual's witness to the gospel.

Because liturgy means the work of the people—*all* the people—true liturgical worship must take the presence of children seriously. True liturgical worship wants infants and children active in the worship space. After all, Jesus had something to say about this. When his adult disciples wanted to exclude them he said, "Let the little children come to me; do not stop them . . ." (Mark 10:14 and parallels). If we are going to be faithful to the full inclusion of all, including children, then we have to do more than periodically have the children entertain us with some cute song from the children's choir. Children can read, serve communion, usher, lead prayers, sing, and do most anything that adults do.

Children, the Eucharist, and Eschatological Hope. To be authentically liturgical, the Eucharist must invite and include all, including children. In our worldwide church today, church bodies and congregations within those church bodies have differing practices on the age when people begin to receive the elements of communion. In the congregation I serve, we practice open communion. We believe that a communion table that is inclusive of all is biblically and theologically faithful.[1] Since moving to totally open communion in 1997, the discussion that this policy has generated and the actual practice of it in our life together have served to amplify our proclamation that the gospel is not a deal. Being of the right age or having the right understanding is not a prerequisite that earns the privilege of coming to the meal. The practice of open communion has profoundly affected our congregational ethos in terms of living in the joy of God's radical inclusiveness. Perhaps most important, the imagery of all coming to the table—adults and children, the elderly in wheelchairs, infants in their parent's arms, and strangers in our midst—is authentic to the story that has grasped us. In a postmodern age that is drawn to the power of imagery, the living witness of a congregation gathered for worship in which all participate is perhaps the most powerful image imaginable.

A sad reality in many congregations is that children are excluded from worship for market-driven or other consumer needs. Many congregations hold Sunday school simultaneously with worship. The theory is that kids can go learn about God while their parents go to worship. Admittedly, it's hard to sit and listen to a sermon when a kid is squirming next to you or a baby is crying. The other advantage of this simultaneous packaging is that a congregation can supposedly reach more people. Some church-growth proponents argue for there to be as any many worship services as possible on Sunday mornings. Moreover, because worship and Sunday school happen simultaneously, this arrangement is very inviting to families with young children—families who may only want to give the church an hour of their time each week. Sunday school is presumably for children; worship is for adults.

This practice of holding Sunday school concurrent with worship is a technical solution to a perceived problem that carries a very high cost. Sunday school is not worship. Given the primacy of worship, and if folks perceive that they have only one hour to give the church, that hour should be worship. For all the reasons already argued in this book, worship is essential for the witness and formation of the people of God. If we view worship as something that "we want to get something out of," then we are going to view it from a consumer standpoint. If worship is our witness and if we want our children to have faith and to own the church's story as their own, we will do whatever we can to include them fully in worship. The most critical aspect that determines whether a child will develop faith, inculcate a biblical and theological worldview that endures and takes on greater form as an adult, and stay immersed in the church or return to the church after an absence during college and early adult years is *not* Sunday school. It is being in worship as a child. The research on this matter is compelling.[2]

In order to address the challenge of small children sitting through a sermon, many congregations have something called "children's church," where children leave the worship center at the time of the sermon for an age-appropriate activity of music, drama, or storytelling and return for participation in the liturgy of the meal. This is a good win-win solution.

If the agenda for adding an additional worship service is genuinely to reach more people, then perhaps congregations might look for opportunities at other times. In our 24/7 world, many are discovering ways to reach people at virtually any time of the week.

Worship Architecture. Liturgy is not one style among many. Liturgy is the substance of worship that is fully participatory by all. In the congregation I serve, we generally use the Revised Common Lectionary, naming the liturgical day (such as "The Fifth Sunday in Easter"), and mostly use the appointed Prayer of the Day or an adaptation of it. We like following a predictable liturgical form of worship—from gathering right to the service of the Word, to the Eucharist, to the sending out into the world. These practices serve to remind us that we are linked to a wider witness of the whole church in the world. We are not just "doing our own thing." Yet there are elements in our own worship where we do engage in practices that speak to the formation of our own cultural ethos as a congregation. We write a lot of our own pieces of the service that speak more authentically to us or reinforce the theme for the day. We write our own hymnodies. We are also adamant that we do not reinforce individualistic and consumer approaches to worship. We do not have worship services designated as "traditional," "contemporary," and the like. We do not like those labels. We do not want to create allegiances to certain services and engage in the worship wars that such allegiances often create. All of our worship services endeavor to include over time the fullest witness of God's people. So, one week at one service, worshipers may experience brass, strings, organ, piano, a mass choir, and hymnody that has survived the test of several generations. At that same hour the following week, worshipers may experience vocalists on microphones, drums, guitars, keyboard, and brass with songs that have been written only in the last ten to twenty years. All services attempt to include the leadership of people of all ages. All worship services are indigenous to the suburban culture of Littleton, Colorado. I share these aspects of our worship life not to be prescriptive but simply to describe what we do. You will need to examine what is most authentic and indigenous in your setting.

When there are appropriate songs for the themes of the day that are overly burdened with "I" and "me" language, we change the wording to "we" and "us," with permissions and adaptations so noted in the credits. Also, songs that seemingly focus on the worshiper and what a great job the worshiper is doing do not make the cut. We do not sing, "I will worship, I will praise, I will bow down" and such. Worship is not about us. It is about God. Rather, we choose to sing, "You alone are the Lord; you alone are the Most High," and the like.

In creating our own materials for our congregation, some of the material is intentional in creating a community ethos that speaks to our understanding of our witness. For example, our calls to worship almost invariably end with the leader saying, "O Jesus thank you for this place," and the congregation responding with, "That is always filled with your grace!" As we celebrate the Eucharist and issue the invitation to the table, the celebrant ties the invitation together with the themes of the day and invites all, saying something like, "You don't have to be a member of this congregation. You don't have to be a Lutheran. You don't even have to get what's been going on here. The gifts of God are free!" It is now normative in our congregation for all the gathered people to complete the last sentence with the celebrant by shouting "FREE!" In a culture that suffers from the baggage, confusion, guilt, and other neuroses from a Constantinian hangover, many take the time to tell us that they experience this acclamation as one of the most liberating statements they have ever heard in the church. We consider this invitation of the free gifts of God to be the main welcome to our congregation.

As an example of adaptive transformation that can happen with intentional, authentic church architecture, I share this incident that happened in 2002 with a large gathering of leaders in our congregation. In this meeting, I briefly mentioned that the ELCA was again in a process of study and deliberation over the questions of the level of participation and recognition of gay and lesbian persons in the church. During a break, three people came up to me and were puzzled that the church needed such a process. "Aren't the gifts of God free?" was their question. (And the three were actually conservative Republicans!) These three people did not need a technical process of study, teaching statements, and a vote at a churchwide assembly to come to their vision of the church in this regard. They had already been adaptively taken there through their witness in our liturgy.

The Gravitational Pull toward Worship. I once heard leadership expert Steven Covey say, "The main thing is to make sure that the main thing is always the main thing." Worship is the church's "main thing." Congregations would do well to so structure their life together that everything during the week draws people into their worship experience. Some congregations begin each week by publishing a reflection on the upcoming texts for worship and creating questions for individual or group processing. Many of these congregations use this material as the curriculum for their small groups. The congregation I serve uses the coming texts as the material that serves to center all meetings and gatherings during the week. "All" literally means *all* here. The choirs, mission teams, the staff, and other groups spend time in these texts prior to beginning the rest of the agenda for which they have gathered. Another practice is to connect all children's ministries during the week to the themes in worship.

Because the transformational power of worship and the amplification of that power through a gravitational pull toward worship serve the adaptive process, all of these suggested practices show how wise and intentional technical decisions can set up the desired adaptive movement. It is amazing what tone gatherings begin to have when their coming together is always framed within the witness of the church. The main thing is kept as the main thing.

Discipleship

"Discipleship" is a hot topic these days. Congregations have "discipleship groups." Congregations actively advertise for a "Minister for Discipleship." People are drawn toward hands-on experiences that are often called "discipleship opportunities." Books and articles appear on "the marks of discipleship." If there is a stumbling block to the emphasis on discipleship these days, it is that too much of the rhetoric seems to be prescriptive. Discipleship cannot be left to technical approaches. There is no one-size-fits-all formula to being a disciple. Nor is there a fixed set of disciplines that disciples must do, even though "discipline" and "disciple" are linguistic siblings. When I read many treatises on what it means to be a disciple, I am often exhausted. Many treatises are also filled with rhetoric that connects being a disciple with deals, causes, and spiritual self-help.

Discipleship is simply how one witnesses to being grasped by the gospel in one's church, the world, and daily life. It is an adaptive movement. Discipleship is an outcome of the gospel, not a prelude to it. As one is drawn deeper into the identity and calling of the church's story, one's life is going to reflect more fully the manifestation of Jesus. Priorities are going to change.

The stewardship of one's personality or spiritual gifts, time, and finances will demonstrate a deeper investment of the gospel. Some will become extravagantly generous with their money, living modest lifestyles so that they can give the largest allocation of their income to the work of the church. Some will be drawn to giving themselves to working among the poor or with youth. Others will assume a position of leadership or service in their congregations. Others will change significantly how they run their business or conduct their jobs. All will see more clearly that what the market-driven world offers as meaningful or fulfilling is actually quite banal.

The task of a transformational church in a consumer culture is to assist people to discover their gifts, assume greater ownership of the congregation's life and mission, and do what works for them. Discipleship is not to exhaust people or fragment families because they spend too much time doing "church work." Discipleship is putting one's passions to work in ways that promote wellness and wholeness in the whole of life and in all arenas, in the church and the world, for the sake of Jesus. From the days of the infant church until now, the baptized live in the world among all walks of life.

The Church's Ministries

As stated earlier in this book, the church does not exist to meet people's needs. It exists to meet God's needs. Adding to the list of words that need to be eliminated from the church's vocabulary is the word *program*. The notion of "program" is laden with technical mind-sets. When a family gathers together to share stories or play in a park together, it is not a program. It is simply what a family does. The ministries of a congregation—youth, education, fellowship, and others—are not programs. They are simply what the congregation does as its witness. They are part of the adaptive movement of being grasped by the church's story.

Congregations who are still under the spell of the Constantinian synthesis, and therefore presumably clergy and staff driven, will have much difficulty jettisoning the concept that the church consists of programs. The issue that is at stake is one of ownership. Who truly owns the ministry? The clergy? The clergy and a few key "lay" people? Or all the people of the congregation? If the authentic congregation of today finds inspiration and guidance in the life and organizing principles of the infant church, then all the people of God will own the ministry. I realize that in any congregation "all the people" owning the ministry is, at best, a theory. There are those in every congregation who choose not to own very much at all, but the ideal that the ministry is to be owned by all is critical to the witness of a congregation. All, theoretically, must mean *all*.

That all own the ministry has implications, for example, in how youth ministry happens. Is youth ministry primarily relegated to a charismatic youth leader with others interested in working with youth enlisted in some sort of supporting roles (such as providing transportation or refreshments)? Or is youth ministry owned by all, where the role of paid staffpersons is one of empowerment? A cry around many church circles is "We are losing our youth," or "We need to take care of our youth." Congregations who are passionate about all participating in the witness of the church will seldom have a problem with "taking care of" the youth. The adults, who have passion for such ministry, will own it. Ownership of it will mean more than providing "programs" or activities. Ownership will mean relationships and partnerships between adults and youth where transformational mentoring happens. No one will need to schedule it. It will simply happen, just as spouses sit down together to a dinner without someone else needing to orchestrate it.

In today's culture, youth should rarely be gathered simply to be entertained. They gather as an expression of the church. Youth have all kinds of options from which to choose to entertain themselves. When they come together as the church, the primal reason is to immerse themselves in the church, its story, and to witness to that story. If entertainment is part of it, so be it; however, the main thing must always be the main thing.

A congregation's youth are not *objects* of its ministry. The youth are full partners in the witness of the congregation, and just as the congregation owns youth ministry, youth likewise own the church's witness in all aspects. For this reason, we might do well to reexamine what it means to hire or call someone to be a "youth pastor." Does that term honor the youth or patronize them? Do we likewise have "adult pastors," "singles pastors," "women's pastors," and the like? Sounds awfully consumer driven, doesn't it?

Echoing the earlier discussion on full participation of children and youth in worship as commensurate with the church's authentic witness, it would be difficult to name a piece of a congregation's witness—worship, education, social outreach, care for the homebound, to name some—that rightfully could not include partnership with the youth and their ownership of it.

When it comes to the faith development of children, the ownership issue again raises questions about the primary medium. Does the responsibility of raising faith-hearty kids lie with "the professionals" who direct "programs?" Or does the responsibility for faith development lie within the child's home itself? The congregation that I serve has determined that home-based faith development should be the primary medium for faith development. This is not to say that kids and adults do not regularly come together for faith-formation events, but we emphasize the responsibility of the home. We have a cadre of adults who have owned this ministry, and with the mentoring and empowerment of a paid staff person, they develop a monthly series of in-home daily table discussions, with age-appropriate options, on issues of biblical faith. People who have never had a serious faith discussion with their children have not only found this approach to be surprisingly nonthreatening but also a wonderful opportunity for the family to take serious pause, in their own home, to daily enter into the church's story.

Ministries of education are not about information. They are about transformation. In this postmodern world where images and experience carry the freight that it does, when a congregations does gather together to get to the task of education and faith development, the less academic the atmosphere the better. Sunday "school" is probably a bad idea. Remember, it's "just church." Congregations can probably name any number of essential faith concepts that they wish to inculcate into their people. Those concepts have a much better chance of entering into people's souls and becoming a part of them if they are learned through hands-on experiences, story telling, drama, songs, and participation.

Leonard Sweet, a leading authority on postmodernism and its meaning for the witness of the church, introduces an acronym in his book *Post-Modern Pilgrims*—EPIC—to describe the essential elements to postmodern faith development.[3] "E" stands for experiential. "P" stands for participatory. "I'" stands for image driven. "C" stands for connected. It is very difficult to be "EPIC" in a traditional Sunday school. Congregations will need to explore creative ways to be "EPIC" in their own settings and with what works for their own people. Some congregations are discovering that there is greater potential to accomplish this in larger blocks of time away from Sunday mornings. Other congregations recognize that, for them, the greatest opportunity to seize people with EPIC educational ministries is to hold them before or after worship and thus they strive to be richly fruitful in a limited amount of time.

Fellowship and other ministries are also not programs. Like worship, youth work, and so forth, they are also times for the church to gather and to build up and magnify the witness. Important to all of these is that these ministries cannot be owned only by the clergy alone nor driven by them. These ministries should be fully owned, dreamed, and imagined by all the people of the congregation, lavishly using their gifts, as witnesses to the resurrection.

Movement toward the Ancient Future

The purpose of this chapter has been to envision an alternative future with some basic congregational architecture that is authentic and thus transformational. It has attempted to take clues from the ancient church about the church's being and to use them to imagine a church that is at once not really new yet at the same time amazingly new in its compelling nature in our culture today. I've not tried to suggest in this chapter or in this book that the moves identified for the rebirthing of the church are an easy endeavor. Most delivery rooms are filled with cries and screams, both of pain and joy. It is hard on both the parent and the baby being born. There is no easy way except to go through the birth pangs.

It takes courage to be about the task of birthing. Some avoid the task out of fear, whether that fear is fear of the unknown or fear of the pain necessary to bring about transformation. Revisiting a theme from chapter one, adaptive leadership is not exercised without great peril. Yet there are congregations—those lifted up earlier as advance scouts—who are thriving in their adaptive journeys. There is great diversity among them, but a constant theme that runs through all of them is a particular spirit. To the nature of this spirit is where the final chapter turns.

Chapter Six

A New and Right Spirit

> Create in us a clean heart, O God,
> and put a new and right spirit within us.
> Do not cast us away from your presence,
> and do not take your holy spirit from us.
> Restore to us the joy of your salvation,
> And sustain in us a willing spirit.
> —Psalm 51:10-12[1]

When many churches gather on Ash Wednesday to commence the season of Lent, the congregation often begins their worship with the words from this ancient psalm. In the forty days that follow, the church enters into a time of reflection for the purposes of personal and community renewal. Lent begins with a confession of our brokenness and our failures to "get it right." We confess to being estranged from God and estranged from one another. We beg God to "have mercy" on us as Psalm 51 begins, according to God's "steadfast love." As we live through Lent, attention is often paid to baptism and its conference of the death and resurrection of Jesus. We are confronted with the startling reality that we cannot save ourselves. We become aware that our own promises to "do better" have no more substance than many of the New Year's resolutions we make. We have no strategic plan. We have no new program. Only God can save us. Only God can change our state of affairs. Easter awaits us. The stone will be rolled away. Hope will be born again.

As we wrestle with what it means to be an authentic church in today's consumer culture, hopefully we are aware that God is rolling the stone away again. The albatross of the Constantinian synthesis and its hangover is being lifted and put to death. There is a whole new world that awaits us. There is a powerfully transformational ancient and authentic church with its incredible true story being reborn anew and rising. As this book repeatedly has argued, the rebirth of the church will not be the result of more strategies, more programs, or more church-growth precepts. It will be reborn because we will let the story go to work on us. It will be reborn because the Astroturf that has kept the church from the rich soil around its fundamental roots will be stripped away. The rebirth of the church begins with a new and right spirit born of God.

Charismatic Leadership Is Passé

There still exist church theorists who boil down the question of the vitality of the church to charismatic leadership. This group argues that churches with charismatic leaders will thrive because people are attracted to them and pay attention to them. Forget about all the seminars, church-renewal initiatives, and the like. It's all about leadership. Get the right leader, preferably charismatic, and everything else will take care of itself.

Certainly leadership is critical in any system, but there is a school of thought and solid research developing today that says that the charismatic aspect is overplayed. Management researcher Jim Collins, in his book *Good to Great*, did an exhaustive five-year research project to determine why certain companies dramatically outperformed others in their industries.[2] Collins identified eleven companies who made the good-to-great leap. To make Collins's list, the company had to solidly outperform the others over a fifteen-year period. It could not just be a one- or two-year fluke. One of his key and surprising findings was that the leaders of these good-to-great companies were not the kind of larger-than-life figures one would imagine. Rather than drawing attention to themselves, these leaders invested deeply in the system. Instead of creating an impressive aura about themselves, they worked to instill the right culture, environment, or aura for their organizations so that the people could thrive.[3] The focus was on having a right spirit within the organization.

A Right Spirit

Leadership expert Daniel Goleman and his colleagues Richard Boyatzis and Annie McKee might be called soul mates to Jim Collins. Their national bestseller book, *Primal Leadership*, also argues about how effective leaders create the right resonance.[4] They also place little stock in strategies and business plans as the starting point for success. Instead, they focus on mood, emotional health, and setting the right tone in an organization. The right mood and tone have to do with creating positive energy, confidence, and resonance among the people. Again, it is all about spirit.

Leonard Sweet, in his book *Summoned to Lead*, speaks about "right spirits and wrong spirits."[5] This entire book on leadership is not at all about strategic plans and the like but about the soul or spirit of an organization. Sweet speaks of "good vibrations." Throughout the book he draws upon the experience of Ernest Shackelton and his twenty-eight-man crew. From 1914 to 1917 the Shackelton-led team survived a failed attempt to reach the South Pole and yet endured to safety under the "harshest climate and severest conditions imaginable."[6] That Shackelton and his men were able to survive and reach safety was not because of contingency plans or a master vision. They endured because, as a team, they had the right soul, attitude, outlook, courage, realness, ability to risk, and tenacity. Again, it is about a right spirit.

Bill Easum, in his book *Unfreezing Moves*, follows the same theme.[7] He calls the church an organic movement and argues that organic movements "embody the spirit of the founder."[8] The founder of the church is Jesus the Christ. The church should reflect his spirit. In his book Easum makes the compelling argument that in this day and age churches should recruit staff not on the basis of their credentials or skill sets but because of their passion quotient.[9] Again, it's a spirit thing.

My own experience tells me that organizations thrive when they have a right spirit and suffer when they do not. My experience further tells me that congregations thrive—regardless of location, population and demographic trends, denominational or nondenominational brand—when there is a spirit present that reflects the church's story. If God has indeed raised the crucified Jesus from the dead, and if the tomb is indeed empty, the spirit that lives within a congregation will invariably be hopeful, thankful, joyful, honest, and expectant. The leaders and the people will collectively reflect such a spirit.

I have also seen congregations in some of the most promising settings struggle and suffer under leadership that is bright and theologically astute but who are controllers, quick to find fault, and exude negativity and cynicism about virtually everything. I have seen certain people bring a funk or a sickness to church staffs that were once courageous, healthy, passionate, synergistic, and possessing contagious enthusiasm. The whole system, staff and congregation, gets sick because someone has come onto the staff who does not have a right spirit. On the other hand, I have seen congregations thrive that are led by people who have virtually no skill sets in visionary leadership but who have and communicate a right spirit. Remember, "For God all things are possible" (Mark 10:27 and others).

If Not Charisma, Then What?

There has been an unresolved debate among leadership theorists in answer to the question, "Are leaders born with inherent gifts to be leaders, or are leaders developed?" The phrase "natural-born leader" reflects the argument that leaders are necessarily those people born with certain attributes deemed necessary to be powerful leaders—charisma, confidence, commanding presence, vision, persuasive skills, and the like. Others argue that just about anyone can be developed into a leader, that good leaders are made and not necessarily born. Leonard Sweet speaks about leaders in another way: "Leaders are neither born nor made. Leaders are summoned. They are called into existence by circumstances, and those who rise to the occasion are leaders."[10]

The rebirthing of the church today in this opportune time is such an occasion to which leaders arise. In my own experience in mentoring and developing leaders, whether it be the paid and unpaid servants of my congregations, the many interns and residents whom I have been privileged to supervise, or pastors and leaders of other congregations with whom I have journeyed, I am convinced that the most highly effective leaders are those who feel summoned by God to lead in this pregnant time. They sense that God is up to something and that they have been drafted into some form of leadership. In my working with them, I have discovered certain attributes or skill sets that they embody or are willing to absorb. The list below is not exhaustive but does contain those qualities that I feel are critically important to lead today. They embody a right spirit.

1. *An absolute passion for the church and its mission.* This quality is distinguished from a need to be liked or needed or the understanding that leadership in the church is akin to a helping profession. It also has nothing to do with credentials. Jesus' first disciples were lacking in any impressive credentials. Passion here means that people have been seized by the transformational power of the church, are unashamedly in love with Jesus Christ, and are caught up in a sense of urgency about the church's mission. It would be a mistake to assume that passion is readily apparent in all leaders. For some the fire visibly burns bright. In others, the furnace burns internally.

2. *Teachability.* Leaders want to know their growing edges and are open to any process of evaluation. Leaders learn from their mistakes and are hungry to widen their expertise and increase their skill levels. On the other hand, they know their strengths. Leaders are much more likely to find joy and thus be effective if given permission to go with and further develop their strengths. A right-handed person is going to shoot a basketball much better with the right hand than the left.

3. *Leaders show up.* I believe that 90 percent of life is simply showing up—that is, entering into the situation as it may be and giving one's self to it. In this day of the church, passion, teachability, and showing up are much more important than

experience, managerial aura, or skill sets. For passionate, committed, and teachable people, skill sets can be learned.

4. *Integrity*. People are not born with integrity. It is taught and expected.

5. *Courage*. Not foolhardiness but courage. Leaders are often called to make the choices nobody else wants to make. Leaders are subject to second-guessing and criticism. A person who has never faced criticism or adversity is probably a person who has never stepped up and truly led.

6. *Humility*. The transformation of the church is the work of God, not us. In whom is someone's trust? Themselves and their gifts? Or God? The church is a living witness that God is able to do some very extraordinary things through very ordinary people.

7. *Social analysis*. In terms of skill sets needed for today, leaders need the ability to do social analysis on their context and congregations. They need to be able to see and name reality for what it is. Seeing often means listening. It also means to be able to read the congregation, its cultural setting, and to be able to identify and name systems and subsystems at work. Social analysis in today's church would include the ability to discern the nuances of deal, cause, and chaplaincy within a congregation's practice. Good leaders spend the majority of their time listening and discerning, not talking.[11]

8. *Situational leadership*. Having the skills for situational leadership is a must. Leadership is not about having a certain style. The style must fit the situation. Each style is essentially a combination of offering direction and offering support to those one leads. Discerning what style is needed is essential.[12]

9. *Spiritual development*. In terms of seeking servant-leaders for today's congregations, I would choose those who spend much more time in investing in their own spiritual development than in developing skill sets or learning the latest church-growth strategy. The highly effective leader of the reborn church will not be a CEO-type but a spiritual giant.

10. *Team players*. Also in searching out and seeking leaders, it is imperative to choose team players. Doing ministry as a team

is essential to the authentic congregation. Everybody works together like a symphony.

Leaders who rise to today's situation will not only need to carry certain qualities and skills, they will need to grasp the complexities of adaptive leadership that brings about lasting transformational change. Charisma may bring energy to a situation, but charisma alone will not bring about transformation. Transformational efforts often fail because they solely rely upon charisma when what is needed is stamina. Lasting transformation that ushers forth an authentic church usually means the incorporation of the following:

1. *Intentional and persistent attention to the church's ancient and authentic story and its implications.* This has been the exhaustive theme of this book. It must permeate every aspect of the congregation's life together. Perhaps the question to be asked of the system is this: "If we believed with every fiber of our being that God has raised Jesus from the dead, what would our life together look like? What would worship, faith formation, and compassion look like? How would we be organized?"

2. *Communicating with clarity, persuasion, precision, lavishness, and persistence the adaptive move or moves the congregation intends to make.*

3. *The multiplying of leaders to infect the congregation with a new DNA.* Jesus did not begin his ministry by starting a megachurch. He began by calling a very small group of people, investing in them, and turning them loose. Leaders in the movement must enlist and lift up others and multiply themselves in them. Any leader trying to bring about lasting transformation through the "genius method with a band of followers" is putting together a recipe for disaster.

4. *Examining and restructuring all congregational leadership and ministry systems.* The organism must be designed not to manage the institution but to spread ownership for the mission among as much of the congregation as possible. It's the team thing.

5. *Being intentional and disciplined with redundancy.* The transformational effort is consistently addressed and communicated

among all spheres within the congregation. Because of the stubborn hold of the status quo and the weight of the Constantinian baggage, the adaptive movement will need to be repeatedly reinforced at all levels, "This is what we are up to. This is why it's important. This is what it all means." Regular evaluations and critical reflection among all spheres are all necessary. Evaluations are not about numerical success but about faithfulness to the envisioned future and the adaptive moves.

6. *A "less is more" approach to the congregation's life.* Movement away from a congregation grounded in consumer relationships toward being an authentic congregation where all are caught up in the congregation's identity and calling will mean the discovery that much of what the congregation does is unnecessary. Intentional focus is then given to what is discovered as the ministry expressions that truly matter. Leaders will then not need to give any energy to the unnecessary. They will feel free to let those "programs" atrophy or die. The more the congregation leaves the consumer model behind the less the congregation expects others to take care of them or organize activities for them, and the more they own their spiritual formation and the congregation's mission themselves.

7. *Being doggedly determined as well as being patient.* Change always creates anxiety. Anxiety creates fear. Fear brings about urges to fight (conflict) or urges to flee (sit on the sidelines or move on). Congregations who decide to take the courageous steps toward transformation that this book lays out will need to be prepared for some rough seas. It is no coincidence that the context of some of Jesus' most poignant ministry happened with his disciples on rough seas. Do not expect overnight success. If you get such success, you may want to reexamine what you have actually done. Is it authentic, or is it more like Astroturf, as identified in the introduction of this book? Most congregations will experience turbulence, perhaps some waning in participation, and maybe even a sense of wait-and-see transitional malaise from many for a period of time—one to three years perhaps—before the signs of being a vital congregation begin to become manifest. There is nothing about the rebirth of the church that is a quick fix.

The uncompromising attribute that leaders need in this age of promise is a right spirit. This is not a one-size-fits-all caricature but rather a presence and style that embody the gospel that grounds the church. The spirit needed for today is not something that one conjures up from within but is made possible by a God who raised Jesus from the dead and has summoned one to leadership. It is possible because the tomb is empty and will take the form for whatever is appropriate in the setting to which one is called.

A "Tomb-Is-Empty" Ethos

What distinguishes a right spirit in the church from a right spirit in other organizations is that a right spirit in the church today breathes a "tomb-is-empty" ethos. It fits the church's story. A tomb-is-empty ethos is not blind optimism, wishful thinking, or a commitment to be upbeat in the midst of any set of circumstances. A tomb-is-empty ethos takes form when the gospel takes transformational shape in a congregation. It will look different from setting to setting. For example, a primarily Gen X congregation on the outskirts of a city is going to feel different from a primarily retirement-aged congregation in Florida; a very large congregation with resources to support high-quality musical groups and bands is going to feel different from a small rural congregation that has only a part-time organist—but each of these churches has elements of similarity because of a tomb-is-empty ethos. This ethos does not deny human sinfulness or fail to recognize forms of rebellion against God or ignore the realities of poverty, injustice, violence, human brokenness, and systemic evil. Signs of hopelessness in the world are more than plentiful, but a tomb-is-empty ethos lives expectantly, knowing that hopelessness is precisely the arena into which God enters and does God's best transformational work. The conclusion of Luke's Gospel is illustrative here. Two sojourners are on the road to Emmaus (Luke 24:13ff.). In the midst of their hopelessness and disillusionment with the death of Jesus, they acknowledge, "We had hoped . . ." (Luke 24:21). As they disclose their broken hope, they are given new eyes to imagine a risen Jesus who has changed their situation. The tomb is not empty because the body has been stolen. The tomb is empty because Jesus is alive. God has triumphed.

A tomb-is-empty ethos embodies a spirit of hopefulness, not because we are able to manufacture the right schemes but because the God of the gospel demands hope from us. The cross and the tomb themselves bear witness to the lies, hatred, and evil that killed the Son of God; yet, the tomb is empty. God has triumphed. No matter what we face in this world—whether it is financial difficulty, trouble with a marriage, injury to our children, terrorism in our country, lies and gossip told about us, failure, or a doctor telling us that we are terminal—none of it holds the final word. God does. No matter what the church faces, God still holds the last word.

A right spirit is not self-confidence; it is God-confidence. Daniel Goleman might dare to name it emotional intelligence informed by the gospel. In Advent 2003, New Testament professor Mark Allan Powell, preaching at Abiding Hope's Transformational Leadership Academy, went to work on these words of John the Baptist in Luke 3:1-6:

> "Prepare the way of the Lord,
> make his paths straight.
> Every valley shall be filled,
> And every mountain and hill shall be made low . . ."

Launching from these words and utilizing some 1960s soul music out of Motown, Mark Powell proceeded to tell the assembly that what the prophet was saying is that "there ain't no mountain high enough, ain't no valley low enough, and ain't no river wide enough"[13] to keep God from coming to God's people and having God's gracious will realized. Congregations who are immersed in the authentic story of Jesus the Christ and are grasped by their identity and calling in the world have an "ain't-no-mountain-high-enough" ethos of confidence and tenacity. It's a right spirit born of God.

A Right Ethos Transforms

When people are immersed in an authentic and appropriate ethos informed by the gospel, transformation is not only likely, it is also inevitable. Witness the transformation that happens to certain children who are taken from an abusive and toxic home and placed in a loving foster home with a different ethos. So it is with the church. It is my hope in writing this book that you, who deeply love the church and are passionate about its mission, might walk away from this book with a resolve to focus in your congregation on richly using the currency of the ancient and authentic story of the church to inform and shape your life together. If you personally are in need of renewal, then go do whatever you can to be renewed in the gospel and in your call. You cannot lead nor give what you do not have.

Investing in the creation of an appropriate ethos in your congregation is totally necessary prior to undertaking any attempt at strategic planning, mission statements, and the like. When a right ethos manifests itself, things like vision statements do not require a whole lot of imagination or energy. Bold statements emerge more as descriptive of who you already have become rather than what you hope one day to be. Imagine what your congregation and its life together would be like if every aspect of it believed and acted with a tomb-is-empty, "ain't-no-mountain-high-enough" ethos. Here are transformations that are not only possible but are also likely. They fit the "dying and rising" metaphor that belongs to the church:

- Dying to hopelessness and defeatism, and rising to fresh new life.
- Dying to worrying about or obsessing over numbers, and rising to passion for authenticity.
- Dying to self-absorption, consumer thinking, and the desire to have one's needs met, and rising to passion to reach others with Christ and to attend to the poor, powerless, and disenfranchised with the compassion of Christ that has no boundaries or limits.

- Dying to worship wars, and rising to new openness for worship that embraces all.
- Dying to saying, "We can't," and rising to asking, "Why not?"
- Dying to fear of conflict, and rising to welcome conflict as healthy and needful to keep clarifying that the main thing must remain the main thing.
- Dying to fiscal fears and an ethic of scarcity, and rising to lavish generosity and an ethic of abundance.
- Dying to clergy-driven ministry, and rising to ministry owned by all.
- Dying to programs, and rising to witness.
- Dying to negative energy and bashing the church, bishops and judicatory executives, and the seminaries, and rising to an awareness of being advance scouts for an emerging new church.
- Dying to a sense that the church is necrotic, and rising to a new day of optimism and vitality.
- Dying to deals, causes, and spiritual self-help, and rising to a childlike passionate love for Jesus Christ and his church.

Salvation and the Church

There is no more needful time for the church to be born anew in an authentic way than today. Human beings still show that we have not figured out how to get along with one another. Wars, prejudice, poverty gaps, and differing idealisms divide us. We Americans might be free in a political sense, but we are not free from violence, divorce, cancer, troubling teenagers, loneliness, injustice, dying, and the crushing demands life sometimes lays on us. Our schemes and plans to save ourselves in some way through success or materialism or the immortality project fail to deliver as promised. Yet we live by the grace of a God who deeply loves God's children. To value us as children of God and to bring salvation to us in the here-and-now, God decided not to give a lecture, offer advice, or design a program. God gave us Jesus and the church that bears witness to him.

It is in the church where salvation happens. In a world where life has become so fragmented, cheapened, and troubled, it is within the church and her story where healing, hope, laughter, truth, love, genuine community, human purpose, and real life are found. As we who love the church imagine what we can do in our congregations to give leadership, which works to jettison all the deals, causes, and spiritual programs that connect with a consumer culture, and as we imagine wearing the identity of a midwife giving new birth to a wonderful ancient church with its true and compelling story for all, we would do well to put these words in a place that regularly gets our attention:

> Peter testified with many other arguments and exhorted them, saying, "Save yourselves from this corrupt generation." So those who welcomed his message were baptized and that day about three thousand people were added. They devoted themselves to the apostles' teaching and fellowship, to the breaking of bread and the prayers.
>
> Awe came upon everyone, because many signs and wonders were being done by the apostles. All who believed had all things in common; they would sell their possessions and goods and distribute the proceeds to all, as any had need. Day by day, as they spent much time together in the temple, they broke bread at home and ate their food with glad and generous hearts, praising God and having the goodwill of all the people. And day by day the Lord added to their number those who were being saved. (Acts 2:40-47)

Notes

Introduction

1. Loren B. Mead, *The Once and Future Church: Reinventing the Congregation for a New Mission Frontier* (Bethesda, Md.: Alban Institute, 1991).

2. Other titles in the "Once and Future Church" series include Loren B. Mead, *Transforming Congregations for the Future* (1994); Keith A. Russell, *In Search of the Church: New Testament Images for Tomorrow's Congregations* (1994); and Loren B. Mead, *Five Challenges for the Once and Future Church* (1996).

3. For a great read on the ethos and culture of those who constituted the early church, see Wayne A. Meeks, *The First Urban Christians: The Social World of the Apostle Paul* (New Haven, Conn.: Yale University Press, 1983). I will discuss some of Meeks's findings in chapter four.

4. For a succinct and compact discussion on the threefold progression of the disestablishment of the church in the United States, see Diana Butler Bass, *The Practicing Congregation: Imagining a New Old Church* (Herndon, Va.: Alban Institute, 2004), 23ff.

5. Stanley Hauerwas and William H. Willimon, *Resident Aliens: Life in the Christian Colony* (Nashville: Abingdon Press, 1989), 15.

6. I am aware that I have painted a quick and broad-brush portrait of "the Sixties" and that there are differing takes on this period and its implications for American life. For a deeper look into the boomer experience and their values and attitudes, see Wade Clark Roof, *A Generation of Seekers: The Spiritual Journeys of the Baby Boom Generation* (San Francisco: HarperSanFrancisco, 1993) and Gail Sheehy, *New Passages: Mapping Your Life across Time* (New York: Ballantine Books, 1995). Another helpful read is the pertinent material in William Strauss and Neil Howe, *Generations: The History of America's Future, 1584 to 2069* (New York: Wm. Morrow & Co., 1991).

7. Roof, *A Generation of Seekers*, 155.

8. Richard Cimino and Don Lattin, *Shopping for Faith: American Religion in the New Millennium* (San Francisco: Jossey-Bass, 1998).

9. Hauerwas and Willimon, *Resident Aliens*, 92.

10. To get some clues on how many congregations are reinventing themselves, the reader may want to pay attention to two Alban Institute publications: *Can Our Church Live? Redeveloping Congregations in Decline* by Alice Mann (1999) and *Redeveloping the Congregation: A How-to for Lasting Change* by Mary K. Sellon, Daniel P. Smith, and Gail F. Grossman (2002). Also there is Bill Easum, *Unfreezing Moves: Following Jesus into the Mission Field*, The Convergence eBook Series (Nashville: Abingdon Press, 2001).

11. Evidence of renewed mainline vitality that emerges from taking the church's ancient moorings seriously can also be found in Butler Bass, *The Practicing Congregation*.

Chapter One

1. Text by Charles Wesley (1707–1788).

2. Text by Joseph Mohr (1792–1848); trans. John F. Young (1820–1885).

3. Walter Brueggemann, *Biblical Perspectives on Evangelism: Living in a Three-Storied Universe* (Nashville: Abingdon Press 1993).

4. Ronald A. Heiftetz, *Leadership without Easy Answers* (Cambridge, Mass.: Belknap Press, 1994); Ronald A. Heifetz and Marty Linsky, *Leadership on the Line: Staying Alive through the Dangers of Leading* (Cambridge, Mass.: Harvard Business School Press, 2002).

5. Heifetz and Linsky, *Leadership on the Line*, 19.

6. Mark A. Olson, *Moving beyond Church Growth: An Alternative Vision for Congregations* (Minneapolis: Augsburg Fortress, 2002).

7. Ibid., 11–23.

8. Erwin Raphael McManus, *The Unstoppable Force: Daring to Become the Church God Had in Mind* (Loveland, Co.: Group Publishing, 2001), 112–30.

9. When using the word *liturgy* here, I am not speaking about a certain worship tradition. I am speaking about what a church does when it comes together to be the church, with worship certainly being the church's primary witness.

10. Joey Sherman is a member of Abiding Hope Lutheran Church, Littleton, Colorado. Asked to contribute to a congregational devotional booklet for the season of Lent, he wrote those words at the age of ten.

11. This two-year timetable of caregivers moving on was cited by Gil Furst and Foster McCurley of Lutheran Disaster Response in a workshop on our campus in June, 1999. Their research was based upon their experiences in dealing with other communities following disasters—Charleston, South Carolina after Hurricane Hugo; Homestead and Cutler Ridge, Florida after Hurricane Andrew; Oklahoma City after the 1995 federal building bombing; Jonesboro, Arkansas after their school shootings; and others.

12. Jeannette Sutton, Ph.D., University of Colorado at Boulder.

13. For the full text of all the guiding statements of Abiding Hope Lutheran Church, go to http://www.abidinghopelutheran.org.

Chapter Two

1. For more on postmodernism within a context of the church's mission, the reader may want to refer to Leonard Sweet's *Post-Modern Pilgrims: First Century Passion for the 21st Century World* (Nashville: Broadman and Holman, 2000) or Jim Kitchen's *The Postmodern Parish: New Ministry for a New Era* (Bethesda, Md.: Alban Institute, 2003).

2. Robert Bellah et al., *Habits of the Heart: Individualism and Commitment in American Life* (Berkeley, Calif.: University of California Press, 1985).

3. Karl Mannheim, *Essays on the Sociology of Knowledge* (New York: Oxford University Press, 1952), and Howard Schuman and Jacqueline Scott, "Generations and Collective Memories," *American Sociological Review* 54 (June 1989): 359–81.

4. Wade Clark Roof, *A Generation of Seekers: The Spiritual Journeys of the Baby Boom Generation* (San Francisco: HarperCollins, 1993).

5. Robert D. Putnam, *Bowling Alone: The Collapse and Revival of American Community* (New York: Simon & Schuster, 2000).

6. Ibid., 189.

7. *American Beauty*, directed by Sam Mendes (Glendale, Calif.: Dreamworks SKG, 1999).

Chapter Three

1. Text by Harry E. Fosdick, 1878–1969.

2. Text by Martin Luther (1483–1546), *A Mighty Fortress Is Our God*, translation from the *Lutheran Book of Worship* (Minneapolis: Augsburg; Philadelphia: Board of Publication, Lutheran Church in America, 1978), copyright © 1978 Lutheran Church in America, The American Lutheran Church, The Evangelical Lutheran Church of Canada, and The Lutheran Church—Missouri Synod.

3. For the exposure of the crushing problem of Christianity functioning as a "religion," see Robert Farrar Capon's *Health, Money, and Love: And Why We Don't Enjoy Them* (Grand Rapids, Mich.: Wm. B. Eerdmans, 1990). Capon's argument is that religion is the "attempt on the part of human beings to establish a relationship between themselves and something outside themselves—something they think to be of life-shaping importance" (p. 27). Things Capon names as "religions" include attention to health, financial security, romance, and other pursuits. Capon shares three insights that are important for the discussion in this chapter. First, we practice these "religions" believing that they can bring us happiness, happiness

being some sort of control over things that matter to us. Second, the practice of these religions turns out to be eventually "no fun" (p. 31). It is not that they are not beneficial in some way, but simply the reality that we keep trying to "get it right" with religion, and ultimately the religion cannot deliver on its promises. I can count my calories and take cholesterol medication, and I still can have a stroke. I can focus on making the most well informed investments and still lose all my retirement savings—just ask those whose retirement funds were primarily invested with MCI or Enron. I could be the most romantic guy ever and my wife may still walk out on me. The world does not work on a *quid pro quo* basis. We live in a world filled with both good and bad luck. Stuff happens. You cannot jimmy the happenings of this world to exempt you from this reality.

The third important point Capon makes is that happiness is related to stuff that "happens." Happiness is not something we pursue and obtain as a result of practicing our religions and jimmying the cosmic system. Rather, it is a state of being in a world of blind luck, in which stuff happens and in which one is nevertheless secure in the decision that God has made for us in Jesus Christ (p. 40ff.). Salvation and the eternal happiness that is tied to it is not a result of some decision we make, the religion we practice, or the level of excellence with which we practice our religions. It is about God, and as Capon argues, the church announces the end of religion. Christianity is "no religion" at all (p. 31).

4. Founded in 1985 by Robert Funk, formerly of Vanderbilt University, the Jesus Seminar undertook a project to investigate the voice of Jesus in the New Testament for the purpose of determining what Jesus actually may have said versus what was placed on the lips of Jesus by the authors of the New Testament. The result has been the questioning of the authenticity of much of what the Gospels report that Jesus said. Their work has been controversial, both in the method of scholarship applied and in their findings. Many have argued that their work has served to deconstruct faith in the Jesus of the Bible.

5. Two books are especially helpful in exposing the dangers of the activist church: Stanley Hauerwas and William H. Willimon, *Resident Aliens: Life in the Christian Colony* (Nashville: Abingdon, 1989); and Stanley Hauerwas, *After Christendom? How the Church Is to Behave if Freedom, Justice, and a Christian Nation Are Bad Ideas* (Nashville: Abingdon, 1991).

6. Hauerwas and Willimon, *Resident Aliens*, 76.

7. Gerhard Lohfink, *Jesus and Community: The Social Dimension of Christian Faith* (Philadelphia: Fortress Press, 1984).

8. Ibid., 56.

Chapter Four

1. Marianne Sawicki, *Seeing the Lord: Resurrection and Early Christian Practices* (Minneapolis: Fortress Press, 1994).

2. For the significance of there being twelve, see Gerhard Lohfink, *Jesus and Community: The Social Dimension of Christian Faith* (Philadelphia: Fortress Press, 1984), 9–12.

3. Jürgen Moltmann, *Theology of Hope: On the Ground and the Implications of a Christian Eschatology*, trans. James W. Leitch (Minneapolis: Fortress Press, 1993 [1967]), 166.

4. Walter R. Bouman is the Edward C. Fendt Professor of Systematic Theology, Trinity Lutheran Seminary, Columbus, Ohio. This material comes from a series of lectures given at Valparaiso University in 1991. Excerpt from "Like Wheat Arising Green: How the Church Grows and Thrives" by Walter R. Bouman, published in *Like Wheat Arising Green: Institute of Liturgical Studies Occasional Papers 8*, (Valparaiso, Ind.: Institute of Liturgical Studies, © 1992): 23. Used by permission.

5. Wayne Meeks, *The First Urban Christians: The Social World of the Apostle Paul* (New Haven, Conn.: Yale University Press, 1983).

6. Ibid., 51.

7. Ibid., 51–73.

8. Ibid., 73.

9. Ibid., 74–84.

10. Ibid., 105–10.

11. Ibid., 88.

12. Ibid.

13. Ibid., 93ff.

14. Ibid., 143.

15. Ibid., 145.

16. Ibid., 150.

17. Ibid.

Chapter Five

1. People desiring to understand the biblical and theological rationale behind this practice at Abiding Hope Lutheran Church, Littleton, Colorado may download the document, "Open Communion at Abiding Hope," from our Web site at http://www.abidinghopelutheran.org.

2. For research and studies that lift up the critical importance of being in worship with one's family as a child and this practice's relationship to the faith development of children and their witness in their adult years, please consult the splendid work of The Youth and Family Institute, Bloomington, Minnesota, http://www.youthandfamily.org.

3. Leonard Sweet, *Post-Modern Pilgrims: First Century Passion for the 21st Century World* (Nashville: Broadman & Holman, 2000).

Chapter Six

1. The use of "me" here has been intentionally changed to "us."

2. Jim Collins, *Good to Great: Why Some Companies Make the Leap . . . and Others Don't* (New York: Harper Collins, 2001).

3. Ibid., 17–40.

4. Daniel Goleman, Richard Boyatzis, and Annie McKee, *Primal Leadership: Realizing the Power of Emotional Intelligence* (Boston: Harvard Business School Press, 2002).

5. Leonard Sweet, *Summoned to Lead* (Grand Rapids, Mich.: Zondervan, 2004), 76ff.

6. Ibid., 21.

7. Bill Easum, *Unfreezing Moves: Following Jesus Into the Mission Field*, The Convergence eBook Series (Nashville: Abingdon Press, 2001).

8. Ibid., 20ff.

9. Ibid., 117–29.

10. Sweet, *Summoned to Lead*, 12.

11. There are many good books on the subject of social analysis, but Joe Holland and Peter Henriot, S.J.'s *Social Analysis: Linking Faith and Justice* (Revised and enlarged ed.; Maryknoll, N.Y.: Orbis Books, 1983) lays out a solid methodology that any group of congregational leaders could use and adapt for their own needs.

12. The basic read on situational leadership is Ken Blanchard, Patricia Zigarmi, and Drea Zigarmi, *Leadership and the One Minute Manager: Increasing Effectiveness through Situational Leadership* (New York: Wm. Morrow & Co., 1985).

13. Lyrics to "Ain't No Mountain High Enough" are by Nickolas Ashford and Valerie Simpson, copyright © 1967. Among the most popular recorded performances are a duet by Marvin Gaye and Tammi Terrell and a later adaptation by Diana Ross.